Transit of Venus

Other plays by Maureen Hunter

Footprints On the Moon
Beautiful Lake Winnipeg

TRANSIT
of VENUS

a play by

MAUREEN HUNTER

For Trevor:
With very best wishes.
Maureen Hunter
(Look forward to meeting
you one day!)

Blizzard Publishing • Winnipeg

Transit of Venus first published 1992 by
Blizzard Publishing Inc.
301–89 Princess St., Winnipeg, Canada R3B 1K6
© 1992 Maureen Hunter

Cover art by Helma Rogge Rehders
Cover design by Karen Luks, Design DeLuks
Back cover photo by Randy T. Gibson
Printed in Canada by Kromar Printing Ltd.

Published with the assistance of
the Canada Council and the Manitoba Arts Council.

Caution

Canadian Cataloguing in Publication Data

Hunter, Maureen, 1947–
    Transit of Venus
    A play.
    ISBN 0-921368-29-1
I. Title.
PS8565.U5814T7 1992   C812'.54   C92-098122-3
PR9199.3.H85814T7 1992

This play is dedicated to my father
Victor Horsman,
to my brothers
Doug, Jack, Russ and Scott
and to the memory of my brother Gregg

Transit of Venus was premièred at the Manitoba Theatre Centre on November 26, 1992 with the following cast:

LE GENTIL	Jim Mezon
DEMARAIS	Duncan Ollerenshaw
MARGOT	Donna Goodhand
CELESTE	Larissa Lapchinski
MME SYLVIE	Joyce Campion

Directed by Larry Desrochers
Set and costume design: Doug Paraschuk
Lighting design: Graeme S. Thomson
Stage Manager: Chris Pearce
Assistant Stage Manager: Allan Teichman

Preface

"Sunday the fourth, having awakened at two o'clock in the morning, I heard the sand-bar moaning in the south-east; which made me believe that the breeze was still from this direction ... I regarded this as a good omen, because I knew that the wind from the south-east is the broom of the coast and that it always brings serenity; but curiosity having led me to get up a moment afterwards, I saw with the greatest astonishment that the sky was covered everywhere, especially in the north and north-east, where it was brightening; besides there was a profound calm. From that moment on I felt doomed ..."

—Guillaume Le Gentil de la Galasière
June 1769, Pondichéry, India

This play is based on a true story. There was indeed an astronomer named Guillaume Le Gentil de la Galasière (1725–1792), whose attempts to chart the transits of Venus were foiled by war, weather, circumstance and bad luck.

Le Gentil's work was part of a major effort by a number of countries to establish the precise distance between the earth and the sun by charting the transits of Venus in 1761 and 1769. This was to be accomplished by a method called triangulation, which required that measurements be taken from widely separated points on the earth's surface. To this end, 120 men were dispatched to 62 separate stations to observe the first transit; 138 men observed the second transit from 63 stations. England, for instance, sent a team to Fort Churchill in Hudson Bay in the fall of 1768 and had it winter-over there in order to be on location for the second transit the following June. (The team had requested a "warm and not too out-of-the-way" place.) Another team was sent to Cape Town, where it successfully charted the transit of 1761 but became famous for a very different accomplishment a few years later. The members of this team were Charles Mason and a land surveyor named Jeremiah Dixon. Another well-known transit observer was Captain James Cook who, after helping to chart the transit of 1769 from Tahiti, went on to chart New Zealand and the eastern coastline of Australia.

Most of the details of Le Gentil's life and work during the period reflected in the play are accurate, but I have taken some liberties with history. The real Le Gentil did not return to France between transits. The letter from the British Admiralty which is quoted at the outset of the play was indeed obtained by the French Academy, but for an astronomer other than Le Gentil. Although Le Gentil's studies helped to kindle French interest in the transits, I have probably exaggerated his importance in inspiring international efforts to measure them. Finally, the setting of the play and all the characters other than Le Gentil are fictional, and I have re-imagined the personality and private life of Le Gentil to suit my purposes.

The story of Le Gentil's attempts to chart the transits of Venus is a fascinating one. Most of it could not be included in the play. For those interested in the subject, the following books will be helpful: *The Transits of Venus: A Study of Eighteenth Century Astronomy* by Harry Woolf; *The Whisper and the Vision: The Voyages of the Astronomers* by Donald Fernie; and *Coming of Age in the Milky Way* by Timothy Ferris. The references to Le Gentil's life and work which appear in the play were drawn from these books, as was the summary of his life which follows.

The life of Le Gentil

Guillaume Le Gentil de la Galasière was destined for the priesthood, but while still a student of theology he happened to hear a lecture by the astronomer Joseph-Nicolas Delisle. He promptly gave up the Church to study astronomy. Before he was twenty-five, he had discovered the Trifid Nebula, a bright diffuse nebula in the constellation Sagittarius. Before he was thirty, he had been awarded a seat in the prestigious Royal Academy of Sciences. He completed important calculations in preparation for the transits of Venus, and was assigned to chart the first transit from Pondichéry in India. In March 1760, at the age of thirty-five, he sailed from France aboard a ship called *Le Berryer*.

Unfortunately, France was at war with England (the Seven Years War). When Le Gentil reached Ile de France, now called Mauritius, in

July of 1760, Pondichéry was under siege. Because of the war and the vagaries of sea travel, he was not able to get close to Pondichéry until the following May. By then, the colony had fallen. On June 6, 1761, the date of the first transit, Le Gentil was somewhere in the middle of the Indian Ocean. It was a fine, clear day. He was able to watch the transit but couldn't measure it; for that he needed a surface more stable than the heaving deck of a ship at sea.

To salvage something from his voyage, Le Gentil stayed on in the area to do other scientific work. Based at Mauritius, he began a lengthy series of exploratory voyages through the Mascarene Islands, up and down the east coast of Madagascar and elsewhere in the Indian Ocean. The months slipped into years, and by 1765 he had begun to think of the second transit. Convinced he could obtain more accurate measurements in Manila than elsewhere, he sailed in May of 1766 for the Philippines. Hostile conditions there and the preference of the French Academy eventually forced him to leave Manila for Pondichéry, which was once again under French authority. Arriving there in March 1768, he set up his observatory, studied Indian astronomy and waited. Then, early on the morning of June 4, 1769, the date of the second transit, he watched with dismay as an unseasonable storm blew in, obscuring his view of the heavens. (In Manila, the sky was perfectly clear.)

Shortly afterwards, Le Gentil fell ill. It was nearly a year before he was able to leave India for Mauritius, and another year before he was able, after a number of ill-fated attempts, to sail for home. Arriving overland from Spain, he finally set foot again on French soil in October 1771. When he reached his home a few weeks later, he discovered that in his long absence he'd been declared dead, his estate (which had been robbed) was being divided amongst his heirs and creditors, and his seat in the Royal Academy of Sciences had been given away. He was eventually awarded a special seat, but his efforts to regain his estate were long and costly. He gave up active astronomy, married, became a father and wrote his memoirs. He died at the age of sixty-seven.

Acknowledgements

The poem quoted by Celeste in Act One is "On Platonic Love" by Samuel Boyse; it has been edited. Mme Sylvie's line about destiny in Act One is from *West with the Night* by Beryl Markham. Rousseau's admonition, "No chaste girl has ever read novels," appeared in the preface to his novel *Julie, ou la nouvelle Héloïse*. I couldn't resist using it even though, by most accounts, the novel was not published until 1761. The references to convent life are drawn from *Madame de Sévigné: A Life and Letters* by Frances Mossiker, and from *Les Misérables* by Victor Hugo. The stories about the sea told by Demarais and Le Gentil in Act Two are drawn from *Diaries from the Days of Sail* by R. C. Bell, a compilation of first-hand accounts of life at sea, some of which I have quoted directly or edited slightly. I am also indebted to *Camille: The Life of Camille Claudel* by Reine-Marie Paris. It is Camille's statement, "Of the dream that was my life, this is the nightmare" which Celeste quotes directly in Act Two. Le Gentil's description of Venus in Act One is drawn from several sources, principally *The Encyclopedia Britannica*.

Other books which were especially helpful in writing the play include *Beyond the Reefs* by William Travis; *A Long Desire* by Evan S. Connell; *Starseekers* by Colin Wilson; *Infinite in all Directions* by Freeman Dyson; *The French: Portrait of a People* by Sache de Gramont; *The Enlightenment: An Evaluation of its Assumptions, Attitudes and Values* by Norman Hampson; *The Eighteenth Century in France: Society, Decoration, Furniture* by Pierre Verlet; *A History of Private Life: The Passions of the Renaissance* by Philippe Ariès and Georges Duby, general editors, Roger Chartier, editor and Arthur Goldhammer, translator; and *A Woman's Life in the Court of the Sun King: Letters of Liselotte von der Pfalz, 1652–1722* translated and introduced by Elborg Forster.

I would like to thank the Canada Council, the Manitoba Arts Council, Manitoba Theatre Centre and the Manitoba Association of Playwrights for their contribution to the development of this play. I'm grateful to Hans Thater, who first told me about Le Gentil; to the many friends and relatives who offered comments and encouragement, especially Martha Brooks, Stephanie Kostiuk, Mary Valentine and my husband Gary; to George Toles and Svetlana Zylin for their comments on the early drafts; and to Steven Schipper for his ongoing support of my work and his faith in this play. I'm grateful to the actors who gave the play its first reading and to those in the première production, who also participated in a workshop of the play in Toronto in August 1992. In particular, I'm grateful to Larry Desrochers. He became involved in the development of the play after I'd completed the second draft and subsequently spent countless hours discussing, analysing and critiquing it. His commitment to *Transit of Venus*, his exacting standards, and his skills as dramaturge, editor and director helped substantially to shape, focus and enrich the last two drafts.

Maureen Hunter
November 1992
Winnipeg

Setting

The play takes place in a country home in France in March 1760, July 1766 and November 1771. The windows of this home are outstanding: they soar upwards, dominating the rooms within and opening them to the sun and moon and stars.

The period of the play should be suggested as simply as possible. I like Milan Kundera's words at the outset of his play, *Jacques and his Master*:

> "The action takes place in the eighteenth century, but in the eighteenth century as we dream of it today. Just as the language of the play does not aim to reproduce the language of the time, so the setting and costumes must not stress the period. The historicity of the characters ... though never in question, should be slightly muted."

The following furniture will be required:

> The study: a desk, a few chairs, a telescope;
> The sitting room: a settee, a few chairs and small tables;
> The observatory: a telescope, a free-standing terrestrial globe, a chair and footstool, a table.

In the original production, the set was designed so that the action could flow freely through the study and sitting room, up a set of curved stairs to the observatory. Since space in the observatory was limited and more distant from the audience, opportunities were taken at appropriate moments in both Act One, Scene Four and Act Two, Scene Three to move the action down the stairs into the study or sitting room.

Characters
(ages apply to the year 1760)

LE GENTIL: Guillaume Le Gentil de la Galasière, 35, astronomer
DEMARAIS: 18, his assistant
MARGOT: 36, his housekeeper and his mother's lady-companion
CELESTE: 15, his fiancée
MME SYLVIE: Sylvie de la Galasière, 65, his mother

Act One: March 1760

Scene One

*(The study. 5 a.m. Heavy rain. There's a commotion off-stage, then
LE GENTIL strides on. His outer clothes—coat, hat, gloves, and
boots—are mud-spattered and drenched from the rain. He carries
a lantern and a leather saddlebag. He moves to the desk, sets down
the lantern, tosses the saddlebag across a chair, peels off his
gloves, throws them down and shouts.)*

LE GENTIL: Demarais! *(Pulls off his overcoat.)* Demarais! Get up and
get in here, Demarais. Now.

*(He tosses his overcoat across a chair, lights a candle, opens a
drawer, takes out a carafe and glasses. DEMARAIS runs on; it's
obvious his clothes have been hastily pulled on. He stands staring
at LE GENTIL, who's enjoying the moment so much he's prepared
to spin it out forever.)*

DEMARAIS: Well?

LE GENTIL: I've ridden all night straight into a driving rain and all you
can say is "Well"?

DEMARAIS: We've got a ship.

LE GENTIL: That's more like it.

DEMARAIS: We've got a ship!

LE GENTIL: We've got a ship, Demarais.

(DEMARAIS lets out a whoop.)

She's called *Le Berryer* and she sails on the twenty-sixth.

DEMARAIS: From?

LE GENTIL: Brest. She's a troop ship but she'll get us there all right.

(He pours drinks.)

DEMARAIS: How soon do we leave?

LE GENTIL: As soon as we're packed. Tomorrow. The roads are fiendish, it will be slow going all the way to the sea. Well, what are you waiting for? Get over here and have a drink with me. If this isn't a night for celebration, Demarais, there will never be one in our lifetime.

(DEMARAIS joins LE GENTIL. They raise their glasses.)

To India! May her skies be clear.

DEMARAIS: To India, and the ship that takes us there!

(They drink.)

LE GENTIL: You're grinning like a maniac.

DEMARAIS: No more than you.

LE GENTIL: I am a maniac. Haven't I ridden six hours through the rain? I'm soaked to the bone but what a ride, Demarais, what a night.

DEMARAIS: It can't be true. I must be dreaming.

LE GENTIL: It's no dream, I promise you that.

DEMARAIS: A troop ship?

LE GENTIL: A troop ship.

DEMARAIS: I suppose that means we're liable to see action.

LE GENTIL: Oh, that's been taken care of.

DEMARAIS: What do you mean?

LE GENTIL: I mean that in my pocket, Demarais, right here over my heart, lies a letter telling any damned Englishman we run into to back off and let us through.

DEMARAIS: How did you get it?

LE GENTIL: Delisle got it.

DEMARAIS: How?

LE GENTIL: He wrote the British Admiralty. And damned if they didn't answer! Here, you know English, read it for yourself.

DEMARAIS: *(Takes the letter, reads.)* "To the respective captains and commanders of His Majesty's ships and vessels: Whereas the Academy of Sciences at Paris has appointed several of its members to proceed to different parts of the world to observe the expected transit of Venus over the sun, one of whom, the bearer, Monsieur Le Gentil de la Galasière, is to make such observation at Pondichéry on the east coast of India, and whereas—

LE GENTIL: My God, the way they talk.

DEMARAIS: "It is necessary that the said Monsieur de la Galasière should not meet with any interruption either in his passage to or from India, you are hereby most strictly required and directed—" *(Breaks off.)* This is incredible! *(Resumes reading.)* "not to molest his person or effects—" *(Breaks off again.)* That includes me, I take it. *(Resumes.)* "upon any account, but to suffer him to proceed without delay or interruption in the execution of his design." *(Folds the letter.)* Remarkable.

LE GENTIL: It is remarkable. Unfortunately, it has its limitations.

DEMARAIS: Such as?

LE GENTIL: If we do run into the English, they'll come at us first, cannons blazing, and the reading of any documents will be strictly an afterthought. But we won't tell the women that. *(Refills glasses.)* How are they, by the way?

DEMARAIS: The women? Fine.

LE GENTIL: All of them?

DEMARAIS: All of them.

LE GENTIL: Even the little stubborn one who leads us by the nose?

DEMARAIS: Even her.

LE GENTIL: Good.

(They raise their glasses.)

To Venus, and the secrets she will share with us.

DEMARAIS: To Venus!

(They drink.)

LE GENTIL: Ah! That sets the blood moving. Now, this is what I propose. You go and finish dressing; I'll find myself some clothes that are clean and dry. Then we'll set to work. We have a lot to do, and very little time.

(DEMARAIS starts off.)

Demarais? Don't wake anyone. The longer we keep the women in the dark, the more we'll accomplish.

(DEMARAIS exits. LE GENTIL exits.)

Scene Two

(The sitting room. 9 a.m. Overcast. MARGOT sits sewing. CELESTE enters.)

MARGOT: There she is, my Celeste! No kiss for your mother this morning?

(CELESTE moves to MARGOT and kisses her.)

Sit down, dear, quickly. I've set out some work for you there. Celeste?

(CELESTE sits.)

Pick it up, please, and get started. We can't have you sitting here empty-handed when she arrives. Bad enough you should be late—

CELESTE: A minute or two.

MARGOT: Please pick it up, Celeste.

(CELESTE obeys.)

You look pale. You didn't sleep?

CELESTE: On the contrary.

MARGOT: You don't look as though you have. It worries me. You've lost all the colour you had when you came home. I wish you'd let me mix you up one of my special remedies. Three sips will cure you of anything!

(CELESTE drops her sewing in frustration.)

That has to be finished this morning, Celeste.

CELESTE: I loathe mending.

MARGOT: Perhaps you'd prefer to darn. There's a bundle of socks there—

CELESTE: I loathe darning, too.

MARGOT: *(Striving for a light note.)* You seem to loathe everything, these days, that smacks of work.

CELESTE: Only if it requires a needle.

MARGOT: *(Beat; then gently.)* You can't live in this house and not contribute, Celeste. Not under any circumstances. Even Madame Sylvie—

CELESTE: He's back, you know.

MARGOT: Even Madame Sylvie contributes, in her own way. As a matter of fact, considering her position—

CELESTE: Did you hear me? He's back.

MARGOT: I know he's back.

CELESTE: Have you seen him?

MARGOT: No.

CELESTE: Has Madame Sylvie?

MARGOT: I've no idea.

CELESTE: If he's seen her before seeing me—

MARGOT: Celeste!

> *(CELESTE turns away.)*

I can't imagine what makes you think he's under any obligation—

CELESTE: Did he send down for breakfast?

MARGOT: If I tell you, will you set to work?

CELESTE: Did he!

MARGOT: Yes.

CELESTE: One breakfast, or two?

MARGOT: Two. One for him and one for Demarais. Now that's it, Celeste, that's all I know.

CELESTE: So! They're holed up in there, the two of them. Doing what, I wonder. Plotting how to keep us in the dark!

MARGOT: Oh, I doubt that. I doubt very much if we're on their minds at all.

> *(CELESTE glares at MARGOT.)*

Why do you look at me like that?

> *(CELESTE falters, quickly picks up her work.)*

Is that what I'm to expect now? Contempt?

CELESTE: No.

MARGOT: You think I've earned that, do you?

CELESTE: No! Mother, just don't talk about it. Please? You know I can't bear it.

MARGOT: Celeste, for pity's sake—

CELESTE: Please!

> *(She concentrates fiercely on her work.)*

MARGOT: *(Several beats.)* We can't go on like this forever, you know. We can't keep dancing around the subject. Sooner or later, difficult as it is, we shall have to discuss it. We shall have to discuss *him*, Celeste. *(Beat.)* Are you afraid that I'll be critical of you? But how can I be? How can I criticize you for having feelings that I myself—have had? I know exactly how you feel about him, and it's because I know that I think I can—

(CELESTE stands abruptly. MARGOT catches her hand.)

I want to help you. Can't you see that? How am I to help you if you won't—

(CELESTE runs toward the exit. MARGOT stands.)

Celeste!

(MME SYLVIE enters, nearly colliding with CELESTE.)

MME SYLVIE: Celeste.

(CELESTE tries to move past but MME SYLVIE puts out a hand and stops her.)

How are you this morning, my dear?

CELESTE: Fine.

MME SYLVIE: You say that as though you'd bitten the word from a bulb of garlic. Where are you off to, in such a hurry?

(CELESTE shrugs.)

Then perhaps you'll stay. I could do with a little of your impertinence this morning. It always brightens my outlook.

MARGOT: Don't encourage her, please.

MME SYLVIE: *(To CELESTE.)* Will you?

MARGOT: Of course she'll stay. She'll be happy to. *(Sits.)* Come and sit down, Celeste.

(CELESTE sits. MME SYLVIE turns to the windows.)

MME SYLVIE: Look at it, would you? If it would only rain again, instead of hanging there. I have no stomach for this kind of weather, it's so ...

MARGOT: Dreary.

MME SYLVIE: I was going to say so English. *(Sits.)* Well, what do we have this morning, mending? Oh, joy.

(She takes up her mending.)

MARGOT: There's no need for you to do that, Madame, if you'd rather not, now that Celeste is here. They did teach her something at the convent, you know. She sews quite a fine seam, when she puts her mind to it. And she's anxious to keep her hand in.

MME SYLVIE: Are you, Celeste?

CELESTE: If you want to know the truth, I—

MARGOT: Spare us the truth, Celeste, would you ... on such an English day?

(CELESTE takes up her work. Silence.)

MME SYLVIE: When I was at the convent—of course, that was long ago, almost in the last century—they didn't teach us much of anything. A little Catechism. How to scrawl a letter of condolence. How to raise one's voice in song, preferably religious. How to enter a salon gracefully, and leave it tactfully. That was about it. I spent more time being punished than I ever spent at learning. I remember having to make the sign of the cross on the chapel floor, by licking the stones with my tongue. That was for breaking the silence. And if I grimaced, I had to do it again—for wincing in the face of the Lord. *(Laughs.)* Well, I did a lot of wincing, I can tell you. That's what saved me.

CELESTE: Saved you, Madame?

MME SYLVIE: From the convent. I was deemed unfit for God, and sent home. My sisters were not so fortunate. There's a lesson in that, which I assure you I have not forgotten. *(Beat.)* I'm surprised at you, Margot. You're not going to let that pass?

MARGOT: Let—what pass, Madame?

MME SYLVIE: Ah.

(She glances from MARGOT to CELESTE.)

I suppose you know my son is back.

CELESTE: Have you seen him?

MME SYLVIE: He rode all night from Paris, if you can imagine, through that rain. Offered himself up as an open invitation to thieves. Risked his neck, his health and his horse ... the roads, I understand, are dreadful.

CELESTE: But have you seen him?

MME SYLVIE: No, Celeste, I haven't. I imagine he'll come looking for us in his own good time.

CELESTE: I don't see why we should have to sit and wait until it suits him to see us.

MARGOT: Celeste!

CELESTE: Well, after all, there are three of us and only one of him.

MARGOT: Forgive her, Madame, she—

MME SYLVIE: *(Overlapping.)* She has a point. I confess to feeling a little annoyed with him myself. Not only annoyed, but curious. What do you suppose has happened?

CELESTE: I think he's got a ship.

(For a moment, everything stops.)

MARGOT: Surely not. Where would he get a ship, in wartime? *(To MME SYLVIE.)* That would be next to impossible.

CELESTE: Not for him.

MARGOT: Even for him. That's a wild guess, nothing more. She has no way of knowing, Madame.

CELESTE: He's got a ship, I can feel it.

MARGOT: Please, Celeste! This is the last thing Madame Sylvie wants to hear.

MME SYLVIE: *(Stands.)* Never mind, Margot. There's enough trouble in the world this morning, don't you think, without our squabbling? *(Moves to a window, opens it, breathes deeply.)* What is it today, the tenth? And March, of course. In my entire life, I don't believe that any good thing ever came to me in March.

CELESTE: I'm sorry, Madame. I shouldn't have said it.

MME SYLVIE: On the contrary, Celeste, you've done me a service. You've prepared me for a possibility I'd convinced myself I needn't consider. I was so certain that with the war—

MARGOT: That's what we all thought, Madame.

MME SYLVIE: But you see, I should have known. Once he'd made up his mind, he'd hardly let a little thing like a war stop him.

CELESTE: What will you do, Madame? Will you send for him?

MME SYLVIE: Send for him? Oh no, I think not. Patience gets the better of the buttermilk, you know. You've heard that expression, I think?

CELESTE: *(Stands abruptly.)* Well, I'm sorry, I can't do it. I can't sit here waiting patiently for the privilege of hearing his announcement.

(She starts off.)

MARGOT: Celeste—

MME SYLVIE: You'd better stay, Celeste—

CELESTE: Bugger him.

(CELESTE exits. They stare after her, stunned. Then MME SYLVIE draws the window shut.)

MME SYLVIE: This has become a very complicated household.

MARGOT: I'm so sorry, Madame.

MME SYLVIE: Margot, Margot, you must stop apologizing. It's become quite tedious. Oh God. Now I've hurt your feelings.

MARGOT: No.

MME SYLVIE: I have.

MARGOT: *(Beat.)* I feel as though I'm losing her, Madame. As though I'm reaching for her across a yawning chasm. In my dreams I see her fall! *(With difficulty.)* I seem to have set a very bad example—

MME SYLVIE: Nonsense. You mustn't hog the blame, Margot. You must share it with us all! Well, you must. We're bound up in this, every one of us, like barrels lashed together and thrown into the sea. *(Sits.)* Come, why so pensive?

MARGOT: I was just trying to imagine where a fifteen-year-old girl would learn a word like that.

MME SYLVIE: Like what, like bugger? Not from the nuns.

(Suddenly, LE GENTIL enters. MARGOT stands.)

Ah, there you are.

LE GENTIL: Hello, Mother. *(Kisses her cheek.)* How are you?

MME SYLVIE: Nearly dead, I think.

LE GENTIL: You always say that when I've been away.

MME SYLVIE: Well, one of these days it will be true.

(He kisses her again, turns to MARGOT.)

LE GENTIL: Margot.

MARGOT: Monsieur.

LE GENTIL: You're well, I hope?

MARGOT: Very well.

LE GENTIL: Good.

(He begins to move restlessly around the room.)

MARGOT: You'll want coffee, Madame. I'll see to it myself, I think.

(She starts off.)

MME SYLVIE: Margot? With a little honey, so as not to burn the chest.

MARGOT: Of course.

(MARGOT exits. MME SYLVIE watches her leave, then turns to LE GENTIL.)

MME SYLVIE: You'll join me, won't you, Guillaume? Oh, don't look so worried. I promise not to pester you with questions about Paris. Or the weather, or the roads. *(Takes up her work.)* Or how well you slept last night.

LE GENTIL: I slept very well.

MME SYLVIE: On horseback?

LE GENTIL: *(Laughs.)* I never manage to get anything past you, do I? *(Leans close, inspects her work.)* What are you working on there, an altar cloth?

MME SYLVIE: Wouldn't you be surprised if I were.

(He laughs again, moves away. She watches him.)

You always seem so restless, Guillaume, whenever you're in this room. Why is that?

LE GENTIL: Mother, there's something I have to tell you.

MME SYLVIE: *(Hoping it isn't true.)* You've got a ship.

LE GENTIL: Thank you.

MME SYLVIE: *(To cover her distress.)* I hope you realize you owe it all to me. I prayed you wouldn't get one—which, of course, considering my unique relationship with God, virtually ensured that you would.

LE GENTIL: It's a troop ship, actually, so we won't be without protection.

MME SYLVIE: Ah.

LE GENTIL: And if we should run into trouble, I'll be carrying a letter from the First Lord of the British Admiralty, which guarantees us safe passage.

MME SYLVIE: Really! How impressive. Will they read it after they attack, do you think? Or before?

LE GENTIL: *(Sits next to her.)* Try to be happy for me, Mother. This is what I've worked towards, since the day I discovered astronomy.

MME SYLVIE: You mean since the day you discovered that the title of savant sat more comfortably on your shoulders than the robes of a priest.

(LE GENTIL turns away; she takes his hand.)

Forgive me. I don't know why I said that. I never wanted the Church to have you; I never felt the Church deserved you.

LE GENTIL: On the contrary, I never deserved the Church.

MME SYLVIE: Well, you see what a heretic I am. You leave immediately?

LE GENTIL: Tomorrow morning.

MME SYLVIE: How are the roads?

LE GENTIL: As smooth as the floor of this room.

MME SYLVIE: Liar. But look at me, fretting about the roads. The roads are now the least of my concerns.

LE GENTIL: I'm going to be fine, Mother. I have no doubt about that. In three years' time, we'll be sitting here together—you and I and Celeste—with all my adventures behind us, and no need to be separated again. Where is she, by the way? I thought she might be here with you.

MME SYLVIE: She was; she left. I don't know where she's gone but I'd relish telling you what her parting words were.

LE GENTIL: I'd better see her.

(He prepares to stand.)

MME SYLVIE: Guillaume. Spare me a minute or two. Your little Celeste is much younger than I am, she can wait. As a matter of fact, a little waiting might improve her. Will you stay?

LE GENTIL: *(Playfully.)* Only if you promise not to wear me down with tears.

MME SYLVIE: If I thought it would keep you here, I'd shed an ocean of tears. I know better. Now listen, Guillaume. I know how much it means to you, to be able to make this trip. I do know that, in spite of the way I behave. I know you've waited a very long time—

LE GENTIL: Seven years.

MME SYLVIE: And that for you it's both an opportunity and an adventure.

LE GENTIL: And an obligation, Mother. I owe it to the Academy, and to France. After all—

MME SYLVIE: *(Dryly.)* Yes, yes, I know all about these obligations. What concerns me is the mess you're leaving behind. You've sown havoc in this household; that's the fact of the matter. And now, when you're most needed, you're going to slip away on us. For years!

LE GENTIL: *(Stands, moves away.)* It's all become a little awkward.

MME SYLVIE: It certainly has.

LE GENTIL: It will sort itself out, while I'm gone.

MME SYLVIE: That's just the point; it won't sort itself out. It's up to you to do that—now, before you leave.

LE GENTIL: What would you like me to do?

MME SYLVIE: I'd like you to clarify your intentions.

LE GENTIL: Surely my intentions are obvious.

MME SYLVIE: To whom?

LE GENTIL: To everyone!

MME SYLVIE: *(With a sigh.)* Guillaume, you're thirty-five years old. You've had a great many women in your life—

LE GENTIL: That's right, I have.

MME SYLVIE: I don't say that out of pride.

LE GENTIL: Or out of shame, I hope.

MME SYLVIE: *(Lets this pass.)* All I'm saying is, at a certain point you lose credibility.

LE GENTIL: With whom?

MME SYLVIE: With women! Come, you're not going to make me lead you through this. You know what I'm talking about. No one seems to know what to believe. The one you say you love doubts you, the one you turn your back on dares to hope—

LE GENTIL: Margot has no business to hope. That sounds callous, but it's true. I never pretended our relationship was anything but what it was.

MME SYLVIE: A convenience? I'm sorry, but you see that's just my point. Look at the uncertainty you've created. Uncertainty, antagonism, despair: the house is awash in it.

LE GENTIL: If I'd known I was going to fall in love with Celeste, I'd have stayed well away from her mother, believe me. Well away! How was I to know? Little Celeste! In my mind she was always five years old.

MME SYLVIE: *(Quietly.)* I'm not asking you to defend your behaviour, I'm asking you to address the problem you've created. I have to live in this house, while you're away. I'd prefer that it didn't function like an armed camp.

LE GENTIL: Yes, all right, whatever you like.

MME SYLVIE: It's Margot in particular that I—

LE GENTIL: I'll speak to her.

MME SYLVIE: It's not my place, you see? And it's very awkward for me, knowing what I know—

LE GENTIL: I understand. I'm sorry. There's some part of me, it seems, that's never managed to believe it. Every morning when I wake, for a second or two I'm confused; I don't know if it's a dream or if it's really happened. It might easily *not* have happened; that's the thought that staggers me. If I'd left six months ago, as I had hoped to, or if Celeste had stayed away a few months more, as she expected to, everything would have been different. Everything! I'd have sailed away without a backward glance. *(Beat.)* In a year or two, she'd have married some nice local boy. Once in a while, years in the future, we'd pass one another in the village, or happen to stand side-by-side in church. Would I be able to look at her, and not love her? Would it be possible? If it wasn't—or if it was—it would be terrible. *(Beat; turns to her.)* Tell me, Mother, do you believe in destiny?

MME SYLVIE: Not at all. Though I have noticed that it seems to get up early in the morning, and go to bed very late at night.

LE GENTIL: *(Laughs.)* That's very clever.

MME SYLVIE: It's not original.

LE GENTIL: *(Sits.)* You approve of my choice, don't you, Mother.

MME SYLVIE: I think it will shock a sufficient number of the right people.

LE GENTIL: Seriously.

MME SYLVIE: I like Celeste very much. I particularly like her spirit. I'd hate to see it broken.

LE GENTIL: I have no intention of breaking it. On the contrary, I'm doing what's best for both of us.

MME SYLVIE: What if you lose her?

LE GENTIL: I won't.

MME SYLVIE: Always so certain!

LE GENTIL: I won't lose her.

MME SYLVIE: What if you're wrong?

LE GENTIL: *(Hesitates.)* If I'm wrong, my soul will wither up and die. And that will be the end of Le Gentil. *(Beat; then playfully.)* And if you ever tell her I said that, I'll deny it.

MME SYLVIE: Why?

LE GENTIL: She has an instinct for the master-stroke—the *coup de grâce*—just as I do, I suppose. Fortunately, I've had a little more experience.

(LE GENTIL kisses her and stands.)

MME SYLVIE: My heart goes with you, all the way to India.

LE GENTIL: I'll miss you, Mother. Pray for me.

MME SYLVIE: Oh, you don't want *my* prayers. My prayers would bring you back much too soon.

LE GENTIL: As long as I've got my measurements, it couldn't be too soon.

(LE GENTIL exits. MME SYLVIE stares after him.)

Scene Three

(The study. Immediately following. DEMARAIS enters, carrying a chest. He sets it down, begins packing papers, books, etc. CELESTE runs on. An awkward pause.)

CELESTE: So! I was right. He has got a ship.

DEMARAIS: *(Resumes packing.)* Finally.

CELESTE: Well, good for him! And good for you, Demarais. And as for me, well. I'm sure he would have told me, sometime before the turn of the century.

(DEMARAIS deems it wiser not to comment.)

When do you leave?

DEMARAIS: Tomorrow.

(The word hits CELESTE like a blow. She tries to hide her distress.)

CELESTE: So soon!

DEMARAIS: It may be soon to you but I, for one, had begun to think the day would never come.

CELESTE: It's all decided, then?

DEMARAIS: Oh yes. *(With a certain satisfaction.)* There'll be no stopping him now.

CELESTE: What is it called, this place he's going to?

DEMARAIS: Pondichéry.

CELESTE: Pondichéry! Even the sound of it is strange. I can't imagine it. I don't even know where it is!

DEMARAIS: It's a long way from France, I can promise you that.

CELESTE: *(Beat.)* Are you afraid, Demarais?

DEMARAIS: A little.

CELESTE: What of?

DEMARAIS: Of missing France.

CELESTE: Is that all you're afraid of? I would have thought you'd say the English, since we seem to be at war with them. They eat their children, don't they? And scorn the Blessed Virgin. That sounds quite frightening to me. And what about the sea, and sickness? Hurricanes, and—

DEMARAIS: I'm afraid of all those things. Is that what you want to hear? I don't mind admitting it. But I'd rather die than stay behind.

CELESTE: He's not, though, is he. He's not afraid of anything.

DEMARAIS: You'd have to ask him about that.

CELESTE: I'm asking you.

DEMARAIS: Probably not.

CELESTE: *(Beat.)* You don't approve of me, do you, Demarais?

(DEMARAIS picks up a book. She takes it.)

Come, we won't be seeing each other for a long, long time. Why not be honest?

DEMARAIS: It has nothing to do with me, one way or the other.

(CELESTE knocks the lid of the chest with one hand; it slams shut.)

I don't think you should have tried to stop him.

CELESTE: Is that what I did?

DEMARAIS: Well, you've made it awfully difficult for him to leave. You don't seem to appreciate what's at stake here. You act as though the whole enterprise were trivial, when the truth is it's unique in the history of science. There are teams going out from half a dozen countries to more than sixty sites. Cape Town, Rodríque, Siberia—

CELESTE: Have I really made it difficult for him?

(DEMARAIS throws the chest lid open.)

Well, he's going, Demarais, isn't he!

DEMARAIS: Thank God.

CELESTE: So I don't see that it was ever very difficult.

(She tosses the book in the chest, moves away.)

DEMARAIS: I don't know what it is you're after. You asked me a question, I answered it. Because of you, he actually considered not going to India—

CELESTE: Actually considered!

DEMARAIS: *(Faces her.)* He's a great man, Celeste; a great scientist. Why does that make you angry? It should make you proud. He discovered the Trifid Nebula when he was twenty-four. At twenty-eight he had a seat in the Academy. He's done more calculations on the transit of Venus than anyone in France, possibly anyone in the world. It's because of his calculations that all these teams are going out. How could you expect him to stay behind? His name, Celeste, is going down in history; I predict it. Because once this transit is over and the measurements are in, we'll be able, finally and conclusively, to calculate the distance from the earth to the sun. Think of it! The final problem of astronomy will be solved.

CELESTE: *(Without looking at him.)* Demarais? Have you ever been in love?

DEMARAIS: *(Resumes packing.)* No, and from what I've observed I'm inclined to hope I never am.

CELESTE: *(With difficulty.)* I can't remember a time when I wasn't in love. When I was five years old, and my mother first came to work here, I used to creep into this room, sometimes, or into his observatory, and watch him while he worked. He never knew I was there, I was always very careful not to make a sound. He was so—certain, in his movements, so swift and definite. He seemed so strong. Then later, all the years I was away, I'd often lie in bed at night, thinking of him. I'd picture him peering up into the sky, through his telescope, and I'd imagine that instead of the moon or some cold star up there, it was me he saw, my face. You see? Even as a child, I wanted ...

(DEMARAIS turns towards her.)

I wanted him to be as intrigued with me as he was with his damned stars.

DEMARAIS: Well then, you should be happy. You got what you wanted.

CELESTE: *(In a sudden rush.)* But not the way I wanted it! *(Turns away; tries to collect herself.)* I keep feeling that I've done something wrong. It's because of my mother, I think. We shouldn't take our happiness at the price of someone else's pain. That kind of happiness is tainted. Isn't it? God would never condone it. Would he?

DEMARAIS: Well, I don't know much about God—

CELESTE: No.

DEMARAIS: But if you're worried about this, you know where to go.

CELESTE: Where?

DEMARAIS: To a priest.

CELESTE: *He's* my priest.

DEMARAIS: *(Genuinely shocked.)* Celeste!

CELESTE: It's the truth.

DEMARAIS: *(Beat.)* Then go to him.

(DEMARAIS goes back to work. LE GENTIL enters, with a letter.)

LE GENTIL: I want you to do something for me, Demarais. I've prepared a list of instructions—*(Breaks off.)* Celeste!

(CELESTE moves swiftly towards the exit.)

Just a minute, I want to talk to you.

(CELESTE exits.)

Celeste! *(Turns back.)* Damn. *(Throws the letter on the desk.)* She knows now, I suppose?

(DEMARAIS gestures towards the chest.)

Well, I'm not going to chase after her, that's certain. A little waiting may improve her, don't you think?

(MARGOT enters.)

MARGOT: You wanted to see me?

LE GENTIL: Yes. Sit down, would you? *(To DEMARAIS.)* That's a list of instructions, for my solicitor. I want you to take it to him. Do it now, Demarais.

(DEMARAIS takes the letter, exits. LE GENTIL sits at the desk, glances through a ledger. He avoids meeting MARGOT's eyes.)

You got my list?

MARGOT: Just now.

LE GENTIL: You'll manage all right?

MARGOT: There's a great deal to do, and very little time—

(LE GENTIL makes an impatient gesture.)

We'll manage. *(Beat; then timidly.)* It's going to be a long three years, Guillaume.

LE GENTIL: Now listen, Margot, there's something I have to say to you. I should have said it weeks ago, but I thought—*(Breaks off, turns away.)* Well. Something unforeseen has happened, something rather strange, I'm ...

MARGOT: It must be strange indeed. I don't believe I've ever seen you at a loss for words.

LE GENTIL: I'm in love with your daughter, and I intend to marry her when I return. With your blessing, I hope. There, that's it, that's all of it.

(A very awkward silence.)

You expected this, I think.

MARGOT: No.

LE GENTIL: I thought Celeste might have—

MARGOT: Not at all.

LE GENTIL: Or that you would assume—

MARGOT: Assume? What should I assume? Clearly, she's infatuated with you but I'm hardly in a position to condemn her for that. And as for you, well. It didn't occur to me—*(Breaks off; beat.)* Have you told her? Yes, of course you have. She knows perfectly well that you intend to marry her. And Madame your mother, she knows as well?

LE GENTIL: Yes.

MARGOT: Everyone knows! Everyone's known all along, apparently. Except me.

(He begins to move irritably around the room.)

But now you've told me. Now, on the eve of your departure. Why? If it wasn't necessary to tell me before—

LE GENTIL: It seemed important to clarify things.

MARGOT: Important to whom? Celeste?

LE GENTIL: To Mother.

MARGOT: Ah! She put you up to it.

LE GENTIL: She asked me to speak to you, yes.

MARGOT: Otherwise you wouldn't have bothered.

LE GENTIL: Definitely not. Better a hurricane at sea, than this!

MARGOT: *(With a little laugh.)* Poor Guillaume. I suppose I am behaving badly. Like a wife, in fact. When in reality it seems my role is to be that of mother-in-law.

>   *(Instinctively, he moves to touch her.)*

Don't.

LE GENTIL: Please, I—

MARGOT: Don't touch me.

LE GENTIL: For God's sake, Margot, you *had* to know!

MARGOT: How? How could I possibly know, when no one would speak to me? Every time your name comes up, she flies out of the room. Every time I look at you, you turn away.

LE GENTIL: You could have asked. You could have come to me at any time—

MARGOT: As you could have come to me.

LE GENTIL: *(Turns away.)* I was negligent, obviously.

MARGOT: I was blind!

LE GENTIL: I swear to you, Margot, on everything that's holy: this is the last thing I ever would have dreamt I'd have to tell you.

>   *(He moves to the windows and stands with his back to her. Several beats.)*

MARGOT: You haven't touched her. Have you?

LE GENTIL: Margot—

MARGOT: No, of course you haven't. Another man—one of those mincing, scented courtiers you so enjoy mocking—a man like that wouldn't hesitate. Out of the mother's bed, into the daughter's! For you, of course, that would be out of the question. No doubt that makes her even more appealing.

LE GENTIL: What are you saying?

MARGOT: Oh, Guillaume, I know you so well. It's not the aim that intrigues you, it's the quest. And it's a meagre quest indeed without an obstacle.

LE GENTIL: *(Moves abruptly downstage.)* I refuse to go on with this conversation. You have no idea what you're saying.

MARGOT: Haven't I?

LE GENTIL: I've had enough women in my life, I assure you, to know when I've found one worth waiting for!

(MARGOT faces him.)

I'm sorry. Margot I'm sorry, but I'm—

MARGOT: This is my daughter we're talking about. This is my Celeste, my jewel! You want me to believe that you love her. How can I? How can I believe that a man in your position—

LE GENTIL: As to that—

MARGOT: With your experience could fall head over heels in love with a—*(Breaks off.)* My God, Guillaume. She's so young!

LE GENTIL: I'm aware of that, believe me. That's why I think it's just as well I'm going away. By the time I get back—

MARGOT: So young, and so impetuous.

LE GENTIL: She's a little impetuous—

MARGOT: Very.

LE GENTIL: Yes, all right, she's very young and very impetuous. That doesn't change anything.

MARGOT: I won't have her tossed aside, like last week's lettuce. Not my Celeste. She's—

LE GENTIL: Enough! Enough of this. I'm not a weather vane, spinning in the wind. I've told you my intentions; now you can plan around them. Do you understand?

MARGOT: Perfectly.

LE GENTIL: Good.

(Realizing she's been dismissed, MARGOT turns to leave.)

Margot, I—wouldn't want to leave here tomorrow knowing you felt that I'd misled you in some way. I haven't done that, have I?

MARGOT: No.

LE GENTIL: You're sure?

MARGOT: Quite.

LE GENTIL: Good. Thank God for that. I have your blessing, then?

MARGOT: Pardon me?

LE GENTIL: On my marriage to your daughter.

MARGOT: *(Beat.)* What have I ever denied you?

> *(She exits. He stares after her, briefly, then moves to the stairs leading to the observatory and climbs them, two at a time. As he does so, the light begins to change.)*

Scene Four

> *(The observatory and the stairs leading up to it. The next day, 4 a.m. Moonlight spills through the windows. LE GENTIL stands staring at the sky. He is fully dressed but instead of a jacket there's a robe across his shoulders. CELESTE appears at the foot of the stairs, wearing a nightgown and carrying a candle. She stares up towards the observatory, hesitates, gathers her courage and climbs the stairs. She enters the room quietly and stands motionless, staring at LE GENTIL, who senses her presence and turns. He stares at her for a long moment, then lets out a breath.)*

LE GENTIL: Well, look at you. Look at me! And they say that God has no sense of humour.

CELESTE: I don't—

LE GENTIL: Understand? I think you do. *(Moves downstage.)* Come and sit down.

CELESTE: I only came to—

LE GENTIL: I know why you came. *(Points to a chair.)* Sit.

> *(She obeys.)*

I sent for you today, Celeste. Three times. Three times you didn't come.

CELESTE: I know. I'm sorry, I was—*(Breaks off.)*

LE GENTIL: Well?

CELESTE: I was sulking.

LE GENTIL: Why?

CELESTE: Why not? I do it pretty well.

LE GENTIL: You were sulking because I'm going away.

CELESTE: No, not because of that.

LE GENTIL: Because ...

CELESTE: Because I want to be the one you come to first. Why shouldn't I be? Why must I always get things second-hand?

LE GENTIL: You wouldn't get them second-hand if you would come when you are sent for.

CELESTE: I don't like being sent for!

LE GENTIL: I know that, Celeste. That's precisely why I do it.

(She turns to him in surprise.)

I won't come running to you, Celeste. Not ever. You should understand that by now. *(Beat; moves closer.)* I haven't slept a wink, have you?

CELESTE: No!

LE GENTIL: Why not?

CELESTE: Why not?

LE GENTIL: Is your bed not comfortable? Is the moon too bright?

CELESTE: I—

LE GENTIL: You have a guilty conscience, perhaps.

CELESTE: I was thinking about you!

LE GENTIL: Good. That's good, Celeste, that's as it should be. But what were you thinking? Tell me, I want to know exactly.

CELESTE: Exactly?

LE GENTIL: Exactly.

(He watches her closely, laughs, straightens up.)

Never mind, I have my answer. *(Moves away.)* You blush so nicely, Celeste.

(She stands abruptly.)

There's no need to be embarrassed. At your age, if you didn't blush I'd be alarmed.

CELESTE: *(In a rush.)* If you want to know what I was thinking, tonight, in my room, I was thinking how angry you make me, how careless you are towards me, how you never tell me things! Today, for instance—

LE GENTIL: Come, Celeste, be honest. You were going to be upset, no matter what I did, simply because I'm going away.

CELESTE: That's not true.

LE GENTIL: If I had come to you first thing, you would still have spent the day up there, in tears.

CELESTE: I haven't been in tears.

LE GENTIL: Your eyes are red as rhubarb.

CELESTE: Maybe I was reading.

LE GENTIL: Were you?

CELESTE: Yes! Why not? Sometimes I do.

LE GENTIL: What about?

CELESTE: What about?

LE GENTIL: What were you reading about?

CELESTE: Astronomy! *(Beat.)* You don't believe me. You don't think I have the mind for it.

LE GENTIL: I've never said that.

CELESTE: Well, you don't talk to me about it, ever. You've never explained to me why it is you have to go, or where. Venus, India. India, Venus. What does that mean to me? I don't understand it and I don't see how it matters, next to me!

LE GENTIL: Then I'll explain it. When would you like me to do that, now?

CELESTE: *(Hesitates.)* How long will it take?

LE GENTIL: *(Laughs, moves to the globe.)* Come. We'll start on earth and work our way up. What's the matter? I'm only going to show you where I'm bound for.

(She moves marginally closer to the globe. He spins it with a practiced hand.)

This is France, you see? This little brown dot right here is Paris, which places us about here. You can move closer if you can't see.

CELESTE: *(Although she can't.)* I can see.

LE GENTIL: We sail from Brest. That's here. *(Traces the route with a finger.)* In three months, possibly four, we'll have rounded the Cape of Storms—here, at the southern tip of Africa—and put in at Ile de France. We lay-over there, then sail northeast to India, to one of our colonies, a little place called Pondichéry. That's here, below Madras. You're sure that you can see?

CELESTE: Yes!

LE GENTIL: At Pondichéry I'll establish my observatory. *(Studies the globe.)* Tell me, Celeste, do you like the names?

CELESTE: Names?

LE GENTIL: All the names of places I've never seen, I like the sound of them. I imagine them like jewels, shining on the sea. I imagine I'll pluck them from the sea, like pearls, and wear them strung around my neck. That sounds foolish to you, I'm sure. The truth is, I've hungered all my life for travel, and I've hardly set foot outside of France. *(With his eyes on the globe.)* Your eyes are remarkable.

CELESTE: They are?

LE GENTIL: Oh yes. To see such detail from such a distance—is quite remarkable. *(Spins the globe, faces her, grins.)* You're shivering. Come and sit down. I'll tuck my robe around you.

CELESTE: I'm all right.

LE GENTIL: You're shaking like a leaf. *(Moves to a chair.)* Come.

(She obeys. He drapes his robe across her lap.)

CELESTE: You'll be cold yourself.

LE GENTIL: I'm never cold.

(He kneels to tuck the robe around her legs. She reaches out to touch his hair, but he catches her hand, kisses it lightly and moves away.)

Now, what else do you want to know? Next year on the sixth of June, for the first time in more than a century, Venus will pass across the face of the sun. I'm going to chart that passage. And my measurements—

CELESTE: *(Sulky.)* It doesn't have to be you.

LE GENTIL: I beg your pardon?

CELESTE: Anyone can take those measurements. It doesn't have to be you.

LE GENTIL: Who told you that?

CELESTE: No one.

LE GENTIL: Then why would you say it?

CELESTE: *(As the truth dawns.)* It's the truth, isn't it? Of course, I should have realized. You're not going because you have to go, you're going because you want to go!

LE GENTIL: It's a matter of timing, if you want to know. Timing, resources. Willingness.

CELESTE: Selfishness!

(He studies her briefly, then moves a footstool close to her and sits.)

LE GENTIL: I'm going to tell you something, Celeste—something that may surprise you. When I was eighteen, and my father was dying, he made me swear a solemn promise. Do you know what it was? He made me promise to become a priest. Me, Le Gentil, a priest! It was a source of some amusement to my friends, I can tell you. But I fully intended to keep that promise, I even began to study for the priesthood. And then one evening, quite by chance, I happened to hear a lecture by the great Delisle. He had just returned from Russia, from the court of Catherine the Great, where he had trained an entire generation of astronomers. I happened to hear him speak and as he spoke, something in the room—caught hold of me. That's the only way I can describe it. Something caught hold of me, and in that moment my life was changed. The next morning, in spite of my promise to my father, I gave up the church. I began to study astronomy. I knew, you see—I was absolutely certain—I had found another, better way to devote myself to God. *(Beat; then lightly.)* What do you think, did I miss my calling? Would I not have made a fine curé?

CELESTE: Yes.

LE GENTIL: I wasn't serious.

CELESTE: You would have.

LE GENTIL: Not a chance.

CELESTE: *(Stands.)* Then why ask me about it? Why talk about it at all? What has it got to do with anything? I keep telling you, I don't understand!

(She moves away. He picks up the robe that has fallen at his feet.)

LE GENTIL: Tell me something, Celeste. Tell me what you see when you look at the sky.

CELESTE: What do you mean?

LE GENTIL: Just tell me what you see.

CELESTE: What everyone sees.

LE GENTIL: And what is that?

CELESTE: The sun and clouds. Stars and the moon.

LE GENTIL: Do you know what I see? A thousand mysteries, each more intricate than the last. Created by God for a purpose: to remind us of our mortality, to challenge and diminish us, to keep us hopeful, to keep us humble. No one, not the brightest savant nor the sauciest wisp of a girl, can possibly look at the sky and not be moved to wonder. What a creation, Celeste. What a Creator! What a privilege to be one of a handful of men in the world who are able to probe those mysteries, and by probing them, help to justify the ways of God to man. *(Stands.)* Now truthfully, Celeste. *(Moves in behind her.)* Do you imagine I would allow myself to be distracted from such magnificent endeavours by anything or anyone? *(Drops the robe on her shoulders, turns her to face him.)* Least of all a little convent girl too stubborn to send me off to India with a smile.

(She looks as though she's been struck.)

Come, I'm only teasing. If you did send me off with a smile, I'd probably wonder who you'd found to replace me.

CELESTE: I could never replace you!

LE GENTIL: That's right, you couldn't. Don't even consider it.

CELESTE: But you could replace me quite easily, I think.

LE GENTIL: Probably. If I chose to.

CELESTE: You really mean that, don't you?

LE GENTIL: *(Laughs, takes her face in his hands.)* Little Celeste! Were you actually reading astronomy? The truth, now.

CELESTE: No.

LE GENTIL: *(Drops his hands.)* I didn't think so.

CELESTE: I was reading about something much more interesting.

LE GENTIL: Oh? What's that?

CELESTE: Love.

LE GENTIL: *(Beat.)* Ah.

(He moves away.)

CELESTE: You don't agree. You don't find love interesting. You find the sky interesting. Why? Because it's mysterious. Well, love is mysterious. You can't see it, even through a telescope. What could be more mysterious than that? *(Beat.)* What's the matter?

LE GENTIL: I'm listening. Go on. Explain it.

CELESTE: I just did!

LE GENTIL: *(Laughs.)* And so concisely.

CELESTE: *(Turns away.)* I can't explain it very well. It's too complicated.

LE GENTIL: What a shame. And I was just beginning to grow interested.

CELESTE: Besides, I'm not sure what to believe. There's romantic love, and that's one thing. And then there's what they call platonic love. I don't believe in that at all, do you? *(Faces him.)* Well, do you?

LE GENTIL: I'm not sure.

CELESTE: You know what it is.

LE GENTIL: I know what it is.

CELESTE: You've heard of it, but never practiced it.

LE GENTIL: I've tried.

CELESTE: You've tried! What a mistake. This fellow I'm reading, in this book I found, he has it all figured out. He's even written a little poem. I'll recite it for you, if you like. *(Recites.)* "Platonic love: a pretty name. / But oh, it something odd is / That lovers should each other view / As if they had no bodies."

> *(She stares at him defiantly, and waits.)*

LE GENTIL: Well. That's coming to the point, red cheeks and all. *(Hesitates; moves to her.)* All right, come on, let's go.

> *(Takes her hand, begins to lead her off.)*

CELESTE: What are you doing?

LE GENTIL: We can't do it here; I wouldn't recommend it. We'll have to find a bed.

CELESTE: I don't mean that, I don't mean—

LE GENTIL: Now?

CELESTE: Like this!

LE GENTIL: What's wrong with this?

CELESTE: Just—suddenly, because I ask you?

LE GENTIL: How do you want me to do it?

CELESTE: I want—*(Pulls away.)* Oh God, I can't stand it. I can't stand the way you always twist me around!

LE GENTIL: *(Lays a hand on her arm.)* Celeste—

CELESTE: *(Throws off his hand.)* You pretend you don't understand, but you do. You understand perfectly!

LE GENTIL: Yes, all right, I understand. You want me to make love to you.

(Silence, which means yes.)

I don't think it's poetry you've been reading, I think it's novels. Don't you know what they say? No chaste girl has ever read novels. It's Monsieur Rousseau who says that, I believe. And he should know, since he's the one who writes them.

CELESTE: I've never read a novel in my life.

LE GENTIL: Good. Keep it that way. *(Beat.)* I won't do it, Celeste.

CELESTE: Once. Just once, before you go.

LE GENTIL: No.

CELESTE: Why not?

LE GENTIL: You know why not.

CELESTE: Then marry me.

LE GENTIL: I will marry you, with great pleasure. When I return.

CELESTE: Now.

LE GENTIL: There isn't time.

CELESTE: Delay your departure.

LE GENTIL: I can't.

CELESTE: You have an answer for everything, don't you?!

(He moves abruptly away. Her manner changes.)

Don't you ever think about it?

LE GENTIL: I think about it all the time.

CELESTE: *(Plaintively.)* Then how do you stand it? *(Turns away.)* Don't look at me like that. I'm fine, I assure you. It's not for me that I suggest it.

LE GENTIL: You were thinking of me.

CELESTE: I was thinking—*(Breaks off.)*

LE GENTIL: Yes?

CELESTE: *(In a rush.)* I was thinking you might like to have a baby.

LE GENTIL: I would, someday.

CELESTE: I meant a baby to come back to.

LE GENTIL: What kind of talk is this?

CELESTE: Would you like one?

LE GENTIL: No.

CELESTE: So definite! And what about me? What if I want one?

LE GENTIL: You're hardly more than a baby yourself.

CELESTE: *(Stronger.)* What if I want one?

LE GENTIL: But you don't. Come, Celeste, I know why you're saying this.

CELESTE: Why am I saying it?

LE GENTIL: Because you're afraid.

CELESTE: Of what?

LE GENTIL: Of losing me.

CELESTE: How do you know that? *(Turns away.)* Oh God. Oh God, I wish I were more complicated!

LE GENTIL: You're complicated enough as you are.

CELESTE: No. *(Moves away.)* No, that's not true. What I need, what I really need to have is a mystery buried deep inside, a puzzle or conundrum that must be solved ... and can't be solved too easily; that's important. But there's nothing like that, is there? There's nothing in me that understanding it would add in any way to any kind of knowledge. No reputations to be made or lost, no seas to sail to find it. So what hope do I have? What hope did I ever have?

(He stares at her. Several beats.)

You're staring at me.

LE GENTIL: Am I?

CELESTE: Like a cow at a new barn door.

LE GENTIL: *(Laughs.)* You don't mind, do you?

CELESTE: Yes!

LE GENTIL: That's unfortunate; I reserve the right to stare at you. How else am I going to decide?

CELESTE: Decide what?

LE GENTIL: Whether or not you're beautiful.

CELESTE: I can give you the answer to that. I'm not.

LE GENTIL: I think perhaps you are.

CELESTE: Oh no, I'm not, I ... you do?

LE GENTIL: *(Moves abruptly to the telescope.)* Come here, Celeste, I want to show you something. *(Puts his eye to the telescope, adjusts it, pulls away.)* Well? What are you waiting for?

CELESTE: I don't want to look at any of your cold stars!

LE GENTIL: Please.

(She moves reluctantly to the window.)

Look through that lens, and tell me what you see.

(She obeys, but immediately pulls back.)

Yes, I know, it's astonishing. Enough to stop the heart. Try again. What do you see?

CELESTE: A lot of stars.

LE GENTIL: And?

CELESTE: A great white ball.

LE GENTIL: Venus. Brightest object in the night sky, brighter even than the moon. First star of the evening, last star of the morning—though not, in fact, a star at all but a planet. A milky white luminous disk of a planet that gleams in the night sky like a star. No wonder men look at her and think of love. *(He is looking at CELESTE.)* No wonder men love.

(CELESTE pulls back from the telescope, turns to face him. He begins to move around the room.)

For the Babylonians, it was a luminous lion that roamed the night sky from east to west. But the great god El was jealous of its brightness, so every day at dawn he had it put to death. And every day at dusk the lion rose from the dead, to roam the skies again. For the Mesopotamians, it was the goddess Ishtar, queen of the heavens, daughter of the moon—or the wind. She was a lot like you, this Ishtar. She was young, beautiful—or not beautiful, if you insist. She was impulsive, and quite contradictory. In fact, she was the goddess of contradictory forces: fire and fire-quenching, fair play and enmity, rejoicing and tears. She was often seen in the company of a lion, and when the lion roared—well, that was thunder. *(Still moving.)* For certain cultures in Africa, she was both the evening and the morning star, the wives of the moon, sometimes the sister of the sun. For the Greeks, she was Aphrodite, goddess of love; for the Romans, Venus. *(Stops moving.)* And for me—Guillaume Joseph Hyacinthe Jean Baptiste Le Gentil de la Galasière—*(Executes a mock bow.)*—she is destiny. What's the matter?

CELESTE: The way you talk …

LE GENTIL: Do you like it? *(Moves very close.)* If you like it, I'll fill your days with it, and your nights as well. I'll tell you all about the stars and the moon and the planets, and you'll tell me about love. And when we've exhausted those subjects, if we ever do, we can argue about how beautiful you are. But not yet, Celeste. First I go after Venus. Then I come back to you.

(They stare at one another; neither moves.)

Will you wait for me? Can you trust me, and do it? You can. I know you can, I can read it in your eyes. *(Lets out a breath.)* My God, Celeste, it's so incredible. With all the things there are to look at in the world, that my eye should fall on you!

(In the distance, church bells are heard.)

CELESTE: I'm so afraid!

LE GENTIL: Hush! Listen to the bells.

CELESTE: Promise me—*(Breaks off.)* Promise me you won't forget the little face of Celeste.

LE GENTIL: How could I?

(He touches her face.)

CELESTE: Promise me you'll come back.

LE GENTIL: Oh, I'll come back. *(Drops his hand.)* God willing.

CELESTE: Don't say that! Don't ever say that.

LE GENTIL: Why not? *(Laughs.)* Why not, you silly girl?

CELESTE: I don't know, I don't think it's absolutely certain God approves of us.

LE GENTIL: What kind of talk is that? Wasn't it God who brought us together in the first place?

CELESTE: I don't know.

LE GENTIL: Of course it was.

CELESTE: Why?

LE GENTIL: Why did He bring us together? Maybe He couldn't resist it.

(He smiles; she doesn't. Beat.)

Go back to your bed, Celeste. Sleep, and dream of me. Can you do that? Can you dream about me while I'm gone?

CELESTE: Yes.

LE GENTIL: Then I'll be with you every night. What more can we ask, than that?

(She stares at him, then turns and runs off. He picks up the robe that has fallen from her shoulders. Blackout. End of Act One.)

Act Two: July 1766

Scene One

(The sitting room. 9 p.m. The windows are open. There are flowers everywhere. Near a chair by a window stands an ornate wooden chest. MME SYLVIE, dressed in her best but with a cane at her side, is asleep in a chair. Somewhere in the house, a clock strikes. MARGOT enters, in a simple dress. She is quite agitated but collects herself and moves to MME SYLVIE.)

MARGOT: *(Softly.)* Madame?

(Seeing that MME SYLVIE is asleep, MARGOT gently adjusts her shawl. She moves to a table, adjusts something there. She picks up her sewing, weighs it, throws it down. She moves to the windows, peers out. She sighs, turns back into the room. Her eyes fall on the chest. She glances at MME SYLVIE, then sits in front of the chest and, with a gentleness verging on reverence, lifts the lid. She takes out a sheet of paper and begins to read. Even her reading has a worried quality.)

Camisoles, three dozen. Petticoats, two dozen. Underpetticoats, two dozen. Chemises, three dozen. Night shifts, eleven. Night caps, four. Negligées, seven. Dressing gowns, three.

(She frowns, pauses. Meanwhile, MME SYLVIE has awakened; she's been watching MARGOT in silence. Now she notices a fly on the arm of her chair. She coaxes it into the air and, as MARGOT resumes reading, picks up a wooden fly-swatter in the shape of a book and begins to track the fly.)

Stockings, twelve dozen. Summer gowns, fourteen. Winter gowns, eleven. Bonnets, eight. Shawls, seven. Lace, nine yards. Ribbon, eleven yards. Handkerchiefs—

(MME SYLVIE claps the book to. The sound is like a crack of thunder in the room.)

MARGOT: Merciful heavens!

MME SYLVIE: Sorry. I couldn't resist a try.

MARGOT: And?

(MARGOT closes the chest.)

MME SYLVIE: *(Opens the book.)* Missed him!

MARGOT: Again.

(She stands.)

MME SYLVIE: *(Examines the book.)* There must be a trick to this.

MARGOT: *(Moves downstage.)* Personally, Madame, if I had to choose between a houseful of flies and that thing clapping-to all day, I would choose the flies.

MME SYLVIE: Celeste seems to manage it well enough. I'll have to get her to teach me. *(Sets the book aside.)* Was I dreaming, or did I hear a clock?

MARGOT: It's just gone nine.

MME SYLVIE: Nine! Surely not.

MARGOT: You've been dead to the world, Madame. How you can sleep at a time like this—

MME SYLVIE: Will he get here any sooner if I stay awake? *(Puts on her spectacles.)* What have you been doing?

MARGOT: I went to check on Demarais.

MME SYLVIE: And?

(She takes up her sewing.)

MARGOT: He's up and about.

MME SYLVIE: Well! He's feeling better, then.

(No response. MME SYLVIE looks up.)

Margot?

MARGOT: Can I fetch you something to eat, Madame? A little soup, perhaps? Some figs?

MME SYLVIE: Figs. Honestly, Margot—

MARGOT: It's only a suggestion.

MME SYLVIE: If I feel like something to eat, I promise you I'll have the temerity to ask for it.

(MME SYLVIE resumes her work. MARGOT turns away but continues to hover.)

What's the matter, Margot?

MARGOT: It's all this waiting, Madame. Every hour seems longer than the last.

MME SYLVIE: I'm sure we'll find there's a very good explanation.

MARGOT: That's what you said at five o'clock. And at seven. We won't keep her in that dress forever, you know. If he doesn't get here soon—

MME SYLVIE: He'll get here soon. Any minute now he'll come striding through the door, just as though he'd never been away!

MARGOT: You never doubt him, do you?

MME SYLVIE: Why should I?

MARGOT: Why indeed.

(MARGOT moves to the window. MME SYLVIE lets her work fall.)

MME SYLVIE: I did sometimes wonder ...

MARGOT: Madame?

MME SYLVIE: If I would ever get him back. I wondered if God would grant me that, and what the price would be. *(Resumes her work.)* He is an old gypsy, you know—that God of yours. He seems to feel compelled to always take with one hand while giving with the other. You've noticed that, I'm sure.

MARGOT: Oh, Madame.

MME SYLVIE: No, you won't admit it, but it's true. He'll give me back my son, perhaps, and take away my mind. My poor embattled mind! Or give me a grandchild—how I'd love a grandchild!—and find something equally precious to deprive me of. He will; you watch. I've been sparring with Him long enough to know this. Well? Nothing to say?

MARGOT: *(Moves downstage.)* I know you like to pretend that you're a cynic—

MME SYLVIE: Pretend?

MARGOT: And I know you like to bait me. What more is there to say?

MME SYLVIE: *(Sighs.)* You were much more entertaining, Margot, when you knew me less. I can see I'll have to look elsewhere now for entertainment. Where's Celeste?

MARGOT: In the garden.

MME SYLVIE: Lord help us. More flowers!

MARGOT: Yes. It breaks my heart the way she counts on him!

MME SYLVIE: Well, of course she counts on him. What's got into you? Just because the man's a few hours late.

MARGOT: A few hours, a few years, it's all the same to him. He does exactly what he likes; he always has. He never stops to think—

MME SYLVIE: You know very well why he's been away so long.

MARGOT: Yes.

MME SYLVIE: And you know why he's late today. It's those scientists at the Academy. They've held him up, poring over all his studies—

MARGOT: Forgive me, Madame. I shouldn't have said that.

MME SYLVIE: *(Beat.)* I have to say I'm disappointed. I thought you'd gotten over that. I used to sense it in you often, this festering distrust of him. I thought you'd laid all that to rest.

MARGOT: I did, Madame. I have!

MME SYLVIE: You *had*, you mean … until that boy arrived.

(MARGOT turns away.)

He's said something, hasn't he? That boy.

MARGOT: No, Madame.

MME SYLVIE: If he's said something that concerns my son, I have a right to know it. Margot?

MARGOT: *(Several beats.)* It's not so much what he's said as what he won't say. He won't speak for Le Gentil, not on any issue.

MME SYLVIE: Well, of course he won't. He shouldn't.

MARGOT: But he's so evasive! He won't supply a simple yes or no to anything I ask. He seems reluctant to look me in the eye, and when he does—*(Breaks off.)* He makes me fearful. I can't help it, he makes me fearful for Celeste.

MME SYLVIE: *(Beat.)* And what else? What else do you have to tell me? Come, I know there's more.

MARGOT: You're mistaken, Madame.

MME SYLVIE: *(With a growing ferocity.)* Do me a favor, Margot, would you? Don't tell me lies, not even little white ones. The last thing I want to have to think of when I go to bed at night is you on your knees to the Lord, begging forgiveness for some silly little fib!

MARGOT: *(Sits.)* He said your son is bound to disappoint.

MME SYLVIE: He said what?

MARGOT: I asked Demarais if there was any danger that your son would disappoint Celeste, and he said he is bound to.

MME SYLVIE: Bound to?

MARGOT: That's what he said, Madame. That was the most he'd say, and that was all of it.

(Silence. MME SYLVIE is visibly shaken.)

MME SYLVIE: What a world we live in! Who can explain it? We rise up from the banquet table, and drop dead of hunger.

MARGOT: Now I've upset you.

MME SYLVIE: Life upsets me. There's nothing new in that. Bound to, you say?

MARGOT: I didn't want to worry you, Madame—

MME SYLVIE: What does that mean, anyway—bound to? That's a cryptic phrase, if ever I heard one.

MARGOT: As I say, he's quite evasive.

MME SYLVIE: It means nothing, that phrase. I'd dismiss it out of hand, if I were you. As a matter of fact, I'm surprised you haven't. *(A definite dig.)* You need to have a little faith, Margot.

MARGOT: You may be right. I may not be a skeptic when it comes to God, but when it comes to man ...

MME SYLVIE: *(Several beats.)* If he disappoints Celeste, Margot, he disappoints us all.

MARGOT: I know.

MME SYLVIE: He won't do it. I don't believe it for a minute. He may not be perfect, my son, but he is steadfast; that much I know. He's written to her faithfully, all this time—

MARGOT: That's true.

MME SYLVIE: Which is more than we can say for Celeste.

MARGOT: That's true, as well.

MME SYLVIE: A man who persists in writing to a girl too proud to reply is not the kind of man who disappoints. Especially ... especially when he's so proud himself. Oh God, Margot. She may have lost him, doing that. I said it! I said it all along.

MARGOT: I beg your pardon?

MME SYLVIE: I warned her.

MARGOT: On the contrary, Madame. You encouraged her.

MME SYLVIE: I did nothing of the kind!

MARGOT: You did, you know. She asked how you would feel if she were to stop writing to him, and you said that while you couldn't condone it as a mother, as a *woman*—

MME SYLVIE: *(Hastily.)* If I said that, I don't remember. You know very well, my memory—

MARGOT: Your memory is remarkable, Madame ... when it needs to be.

MME SYLVIE: *(Looks at MARGOT in surprise.)* Well, well, well! She retaliates. That's a change of pace.

(CELESTE enters, carrying flowers. Her dress is exquisite. MARGOT and MME SYLVIE quickly take up their work. CELESTE moves to a table, sets the flowers in a vase and begins to arrange them. For a moment, no one speaks.)

CELESTE: You're very quiet, the two of you. Have you been talking about me?

MME SYLVIE: Heavens! Such conceit.

MARGOT: More flowers, Celeste? The room is like a garden.

CELESTE: I know; I like it. It looks *gemutlich*, as the Germans say.

MME SYLVIE: It may look *gemutlich*, but it smells like a perfumery. And what's more this fly-thing of yours doesn't work.

MARGOT: It works well enough, I think, when the worker is a little slyer than the fly.

MME SYLVIE: Oh, is that what's required? *(To CELESTE.)* I take it there's no sign of him.

CELESTE: None.

MME SYLVIE: *(Reaches for her cane.)* Well, I don't know why I should be so impatient. At least we know that he's in France. That's a consolation, isn't it. *(Stands with some difficulty.)* He's not off on some desolate island, somewhere—

MARGOT: *(Under her breath.)* Or bobbing like a cork in the middle of the sea.

CELESTE: They're not desolate, those islands. They're lush and verdant. They smell of jasmine, and frangipane. I wish I knew what that was like! And at night, the sky drops down around them like a great bejewelled bowl.

MME SYLVIE: *(Sighs.)* He does write a lovely letter.

(She moves slowly towards the windows.)

CELESTE: He does. *(Carries the vase to another table, sets it down.)* I didn't get that from a letter, though. I got it from a book.

MARGOT: You and your books. If you'd spent half the time on housework that you've spent on books—

MME SYLVIE: Oh, she can always learn housework.

MARGOT: And needlework, too, I suppose?

MME SYLVIE: If she's going to wear her eyes out, let her do it on words.

MARGOT: I know you feel that way, Madame. You've often said it. When, in fact, if you'd supported me in this—

MME SYLVIE: *(Sharp.)* If I'd supported you, what would we have? Two excellent seamstresses, when clearly all we need is one!

(MME SYLVIE turns away. MARGOT picks up her work and makes a show of doing it. CELESTE looks from one to the other. Beat.)

CELESTE: This is because of him, isn't it? Because he's late. *(To MARGOT.)* All your preparations—

MARGOT: There's nothing that won't keep.

CELESTE: The food—

MARGOT: The food will taste just as good tomorrow as it did today. *(Under her breath.)* To those of us who eat it.

CELESTE: You've worn yourself out, looking after Demarais. *(Turns to MME SYLVIE.)* And you've hardly slept at all.

MME SYLVIE: Since when?

CELESTE: Since we got word that they'd reached France.

MME SYLVIE: Nonsense.

CELESTE: I know you, Madame.

MME SYLVIE: I have slept like a newborn babe!

CELESTE: *(Beat.)* Well! Everything's fine, then. What a relief.

(Turns to leave.)

MME SYLVIE: Where are you going?

CELESTE: For a walk.

MARGOT: You're not!

MME SYLVIE: Always running out on us!

CELESTE: *(Turns back.)* I can't sit here, twiddling my thumbs. You know that.

MARGOT: That's no reason to go wandering through the fields—

MME SYLVIE: At this hour.

MARGOT: In that dress.

CELESTE: All right, I'll change. *(Starts off again.)*

MARGOT: Oh no!

> *(Again, CELESTE turns back.)*
> He could arrive at any moment, Celeste.

CELESTE: Well, if he does, I'd just as soon he didn't know that I've spent the entire day looking like this.

MME SYLVIE: Celeste! Your mother went to so much trouble.

MARGOT: Never mind, Madame. She's been waiting all along for an excuse to do this.

CELESTE: That's not true.

MARGOT: She didn't want to wear it in the first place. She finds it overdone, you see.

CELESTE: That's not what I said.

MARGOT: No, you said—

CELESTE: I didn't want to look as though I was trying to impress him. That's all I meant.

MME SYLVIE: That's a very strange attitude.

CELESTE: Is it?

MME SYLVIE: Towards the man you're going to marry? I should say so.

CELESTE: Well, this is an improvement. Now you're picking on me instead of one another!

> *(CELESTE turns away. Several beats.)*

MME SYLVIE: You're quite right, Celeste. We are behaving badly.

CELESTE: Why, Madame?

MME SYLVIE: Why? Well—

MARGOT: It's my fault, Celeste. I take the blame entirely. She was teasing me, you see, and of course I took the bait. You'd think I'd learn, wouldn't you, after all this time? *(Beat.)* I think what we need, all of us—even you, Celeste—is a little something to calm the nerves. Fortunately, I have just the thing. A very special herbal remedy! I'd be more than happy to slip into the kitchen—

> *(MARGOT looks hopefully from one to the other.)*

No one ever likes my remedies. Any more than they like my gowns.

> *(MARGOT takes up her work with a purpose. CELESTE moves to her.)*

CELESTE: Please understand. It's not that I dislike it; how could I? It's exquisite.

MARGOT: *(Touches her face.)* I just want you to look beautiful! Is that so strange?

CELESTE: But that's the point, you see. He's seen so much beauty in the world. I don't want to look as though I'm trying to compete.

MARGOT: Compete? *(To MME SYLVIE.)* Listen to her.

CELESTE: I'd feel more comfortable, I think, in something a little simpler. Something more like yours.

MARGOT: For his coming-home?

CELESTE: To me this seems almost like a wedding gown.

MARGOT: It's not at all like a wedding gown. Is it, Madame. Tell her. She'll listen to you.

> *(MME SYLVIE doesn't reply. She is staring out the window. The sky is ablaze with colour.)*

Madame?

MME SYLVIE: Look at it, would you? Did you ever in your life see a day so …

CELESTE: Lovely!

MME SYLVIE: I was going to say so French.

> *(MME SYLVIE faces MARGOT.)*

MME SYLVIE: She has to know, Margot.

MARGOT: *(Starts to rise.)* Madame—

MME SYLVIE: How can we send her into battle, if there is to be a battle, utterly unarmed?

CELESTE: What are you talking about? Madame?

MME SYLVIE: *(Moves downstage.)* I'm talking about Demarais.

CELESTE: What about him?

MARGOT: *(Sinking.)* Oh, Madame.

MME SYLVIE: Your mother, you see. Just before you came in, your mother was as cranky as a wallbug. So in the end we had a quarrel— over something that he said.

CELESTE: Demarais? *(To MARGOT.)* I thought he wasn't well enough to talk.

MARGOT: He's not. That is, he wasn't, but—

CELESTE: You said he was delirious.

MARGOT: He was, Celeste, at first. And then, for a few days, he refused to talk at all.

CELESTE: But now he's talking. What does he say? It's about Le Gentil, isn't it? What is it? Is something wrong?

MARGOT: Now listen, Celeste. We mustn't jump to conclusions.

CELESTE: *(To MME SYLVIE.)* Madame?

MME SYLVIE: Ask him yourself. He's up and about, apparently.

(CELESTE starts off. MARGOT stands.)

MARGOT: Celeste! Don't upset him. He's not as well as he pretends to be. Celeste?

(CELESTE exits. MARGOT turns helplessly to MME SYLVIE, then sinks back into her chair. MME SYLVIE moves next to her. Several beats.)

MME SYLVIE: You probably think I shouldn't have done that. "Where the devil cannot go, he sends an old woman." That's what you're thinking.

MARGOT: *(With difficulty.)* I pray every night, Madame, for the courage to let her go. Simply—to let her go. Why should that be so difficult? It sounds so easy. *(Turns away.)* I envy you your strength, Madame.

MME SYLVIE: I envy you your faith.

MARGOT: *(Looks up in surprise.)* You've never said that.

MME SYLVIE: And I never shall again. Come, give me your hand. I feel the need of it.

(MARGOT obeys.)

We're condemned to rely on them, aren't we—you and I? We were condemned to it the day that they were born. I have to say I find that onerous, at times. I'd prefer to be independent.

(MME SYLVIE grips MARGOT's hand more tightly and turns toward the window. Beat.)

She has a way of taking the sun with her, have you noticed that? When she leaves a room?

Scene Two

(The study. Immediately following. DEMARAIS leans over a table, studying a map which is criss-crossed with ribbons and dotted with flags. CELESTE runs on, but stops when she sees him. There's an instant of confusion, then recognition. For CELESTE the recovery takes longer; his appearance shocks and unnerves her.)

DEMARAIS: Celeste! I wouldn't have known you.

CELESTE: I wouldn't have known you. You didn't use to be so—tall.

DEMARAIS: So thin, you mean. Well, I'm not as thin as I was a few days ago; your mother has seen to that. Where are you off to in such a hurry?

CELESTE: Oh, I—came to see you.

DEMARAIS: *(On his guard.)* Oh?

CELESTE: Yes, they—told me you were out of bed.

DEMARAIS: Did they? They were right.

CELESTE: *(Hesitates.)* I would have been to see you sooner, but I was told that you weren't well enough to talk. Are you well enough?

DEMARAIS: I think so.

CELESTE: Good. I'm glad to hear it, Demarais. We've been worried about you. My mother—*(Breaks off.)* My mother in particular has been worried.

DEMARAIS: She certainly has.

(An awkward pause.)

CELESTE: I see you've been studying my map.

DEMARAIS: You made this? When?

CELESTE: As the letters arrived.

DEMARAIS: Explain it to me.

CELESTE: It's as simple as it looks. *(Moves closer.)* The ribbons are the voyages, the flags the ports of call. Each colour represents a different year.

DEMARAIS: Red is the first year; that's obvious. And green must be the second—

CELESTE: The year he missed the transit. You'll notice there's not a single flag on India! Then white and blue: dozens of ribbons and as many flags—

DEMARAIS: All those wretched excursions.

CELESTE: *(Lets this pass.)* The fifth year is yellow and the sixth magenta. Magenta is the colour that brought him home! If I'd known that, I would have used it sooner. I'm sorry. I shouldn't talk as though you weren't there with him.

DEMARAIS: But I wasn't. I was on another journey altogether. You look surprised. He didn't tell you?

CELESTE: He said you hadn't taken all that well to the sea.

DEMARAIS: *(With a mirthless laugh.)* Yes. He would put it like that. *(Turns back to the map.)* Tell me something. Why did you do this?

CELESTE: It was a way of going with him. I feel as though I've followed him everywhere, like a shadow. *(Moves away.)* I have other maps, where I've done latitudes and longitudes. Trade winds, navigational routes. Everything he studied and observed. Flora, fauna, soils. Winds and tides; monsoons.

DEMARAIS: *(Genuinely astounded.)* How did you learn all this?

CELESTE: From his letters. And from books. I've read every book in the house, I think, and any I could beg from the curé. History, geography, philosophy. Letters. Even a little astronomy. The more I learned, the more I found I had to learn and the more mysterious the world became.

DEMARAIS: Does he know about this?

CELESTE: I wanted to surprise him.

DEMARAIS: He'll be surprised, all right. I'm surprised! I used to try and picture you, from time to time, while I was away—as I pictured many things in France. *(Indicating the map.)* But I never once pictured you doing this.

CELESTE: What was I doing?

DEMARAIS: I—oh, I don't know. Feminine things.

(She stiffens. He studies the map, unaware that he's offended her. She moves away.)

CELESTE: Would you do something for me, Demarais? Would you tell me about the sea?

DEMARAIS: The sea.

CELESTE: I like to try and picture it, in all its splendour.

DEMARAIS: In that case, I suggest you wait for Le Gentil. *(With an edge.)* He's much better than I am at splendour.

CELESTE: *(Turns away.)* I would love to see the sea. I would love to sail it.

DEMARAIS: You would never survive.

CELESTE: I might surprise you, Demarais.

DEMARAIS: Believe me, you would not survive the sea. That takes a kind of madness.

CELESTE: You survived it.

DEMARAIS: I lived. That's a different thing.

CELESTE: *(Hesitates.)* What about the sailors? They must—

DEMARAIS: Mad. All mad.

CELESTE: And Le Gentil? Is he mad, too?

DEMARAIS: He's the maddest of the lot.

(CELESTE laughs.)

You don't believe me?

CELESTE: Of course not.

DEMARAIS: You've been with him, have you? All this time?

CELESTE: I have his letters. He did write to me, you know. One hundred and sixty-two letters! Every one of them as rich as a tapestry.

DEMARAIS: Oh, well then. You have nothing to learn from me.

(He picks up a book, flips through it.)

CELESTE: I wouldn't go that far, Demarais—

DEMARAIS: No.

CELESTE: But I know he isn't mad! Unless he's changed beyond all recognition. Has he changed, Demarais?

DEMARAIS: We've all changed, haven't we?

CELESTE: For the better, I would hope.

DEMARAIS: Who can say?

(DEMARAIS replaces the book, picks up another.)

CELESTE: Is he—as handsome as he was?

DEMARAIS: I'm hardly an authority on that.

CELESTE: You could venture an opinion.

DEMARAIS: You could wait a while, and find out for yourself.

(He replaces the book, moves to the window.)

CELESTE: He hasn't been ill. Has he?

DEMARAIS: Why ask me? You're the one with all the letters. One hundred and sixty-two!

CELESTE: He might have kept it from me, if he had been ill. So that I wouldn't worry.

DEMARAIS: *(With an abrupt, violent gesture.)* Oh, for the love of Christ! Say what you've come to say, would you? Then leave me the hell alone.

(This outburst shocks CELESTE.)

I know why you're here. Do you want to know how I know? Because you behave exactly like your mother. Sniffing around me like a fish who's scented bait. Here's some advice for you. Try to remember it once he arrives. Think like a shark! When you want something, snatch it. He'll like that, believe me. He'll admire you for it. You may even find—*(Sways, reaches for support.)*—you ...

CELESTE: *(Moves to him.)* Come and sit down.

DEMARAIS: Merciful Christ!

CELESTE: Sit down, until it passes.

(She helps him to a chair, pours a drink for him from a carafe and sits next to him.)

Put your head back. You'll feel better in a minute.

DEMARAIS: My God, you know, I'm—*(Breaks off.)*

CELESTE: You're what?

DEMARAIS: I'm terrified I'll never get over this!

CELESTE: *(Takes his hand.)* You'll get over it.

DEMARAIS: I wonder.

CELESTE: You will. Especially if you don't have to contend with me.

DEMARAIS: I should have stayed in bed.

CELESTE: Perhaps.

DEMARAIS: I was sick to death of my own thoughts! I haven't had a conversation since I got here. No one comes to see me. Not even you.

CELESTE: I was forbidden to.

DEMARAIS: You do as you're told now?

CELESTE: Sometimes.

DEMARAIS: Sometimes?

CELESTE: When I must. *(Smiles.)*

DEMARAIS: That's better. I was beginning to think that frown had moulded itself to your forehead. *(Studies her.)* He's going to be amazed, you know. There was hardly anything to you when we went away. Now you're quite, quite—grown.

CELESTE: Do you think he'll be pleased?

DEMARAIS: Oh, I—don't see why not.

CELESTE: You don't see why not. Try to restrain your enthusiasm, Demarais—

DEMARAIS: It's not my place to tell you that you're beautiful. *(Turns away.)* He's a lucky man.

CELESTE: Not so lucky perhaps. He missed the transit, didn't he?

DEMARAIS: That was my fault. It was. We couldn't get to Pondichéry; it was under siege. But we might have sailed to Java. He could have charted the transit there. But I was ill—I was eternally ill—and he refused to leave me.

CELESTE: Oh, Demarais.

DEMARAIS: I was a weight around his neck from the moment we left France. I was homesick; I was lonely; I was scared to death. He never said it, he never once reproached me or complained. But I could feel his expectations for me fading with each day. *(Glances at her.)* You're shocked, aren't you?

CELESTE: No.

DEMARAIS: You are. I can see it in your face.

CELESTE: I can't believe that none of it was any good. I can't believe that! There must be something you enjoyed. There must be one good memory.

DEMARAIS: *(After a moment.)* I do remember one afternoon. We were somewhere off the coast of Africa. One of the sailors fell headforemost from the mizzen topsail yard into the top. I asked him what made him come down and he said, "Common sense." *(Laughs, this time with genuine mirth.)* I liked that. I like—little things. Le Gentil, you know, he likes things vast. Me, I like them small. I like to be able to reach a thing and—hold it in my hand. *(Finds himself staring at her hand; raises his eyes.)* That's a remarkable dress you're wearing.

CELESTE: *(Stiffens.)* Is it?

DEMARAIS: A dress like that makes a man feel very welcome.

(She pulls her hand away, and stands.)

What's the matter? What did I say?

CELESTE: Nothing.

(She moves to the window.)

DEMARAIS: I wasn't referring to myself—

CELESTE: I know!

DEMARAIS: You have a great capacity for anger, haven't you? I don't think I'd want to be the one who usually inspires it.

CELESTE: I'm not angry with you, Demarais. I'm angry because I'm stuck here in this fluffy fluffy gown, waiting for a man who's always late. *(Opens the window.)* Look, it's almost dark out now. Will he arrive at all tonight? Or will I have to make do with another dream? Oh, Demarais. I can't begin to tell you how tired I am of dreams.

DEMARAIS: I understand that.

CELESTE: Do you? *(Faces him.)* I wonder. I wonder what you'd say if I were to tell you that I've dreamt of him every night since he's been gone.

DEMARAIS: I'd say that's—quite a feat.

CELESTE: The curé doesn't approve. He thinks I should dream of salvation. I dream of Le Gentil. And in the morning, do you know what I do? I open the little chest where I keep his letters and read them all again. I've committed them to memory.

DEMARAIS: All of them?

CELESTE: All of them. But I read them anyway because I like to study the handwriting, to imagine him forming each letter. Everything he touches, everything his eye falls on is beautiful to me. Do you think that's wrong?

DEMARAIS: *(Hesitates.)* Not necessarily.

CELESTE: The curé does. *(Moves away from the window.)* The curé has for some time denied me the Holy Sacrament—because of Le Gentil.

(Several beats.)

DEMARAIS: Listen to me, Celeste. I know how you feel because there was a time when I felt the same way. I wanted to be like him in every way, to stride across the world with all that energy and optimism. To light a fire in everyone I met. But I've learned—*(Breaks off; considers.)* I've learned that only God is perfect—

CELESTE: Well, of course—

DEMARAIS: And that it's wrong to look for God in Le Gentil. It's wrong, Celeste, and what's more it's not fair. To him, or to you.

CELESTE: What are you saying?

DEMARAIS: He's a man, like any other—

CELESTE: He's not like any other.

DEMARAIS: He's a man, Celeste. Sometimes he'll exceed your expectations; sometimes he'll fall short. If you expect it to be otherwise—*(Breaks off; turns away.)* Don't expect it to be otherwise.

(He pulls himself out of his chair.)

CELESTE: Where are you going?

DEMARAIS: Back to bed.

CELESTE: Now? You say this, and then walk away?

DEMARAIS: I can't say any more, Celeste. There was a time I wouldn't have said this much. There was a time you couldn't have pried a word against him from my mouth. But I've come to see the world for what it is, and I know that sometimes—sometimes—there's more beauty in a little act of kindness than in all the splendour of the universe.

(DEMARAIS starts off.)

CELESTE: You think you've done this out of kindness? You're fooling yourself. It's not kindness, Demarais, it's jealousy.

(DEMARAIS stops moving.)

You're jealous of him, because you know in your heart that you're not like him at all!

DEMARAIS: *(Faces her.)* That's right. That's absolutely right. I'm not like him, at all. At first, when I first understood that, I thought I'd die of shame. Not any more. Because I've decided that God planned for this. He knew all along there'd be little men, as well as great. He made room in His heart for both.

CELESTE: Demarais, I didn't—

DEMARAIS: After all, if He could imagine the universe, He could certainly imagine me!

(DEMARAIS exits. For a while, CELESTE stares after him. Then she moves to the window and closes it. She moves to the map and covers it with a cloth. Finally she starts off, but as she nears the stairs leading to the observatory, she stops moving and turns towards them, as though drawn by an irresistible force.)

Scene Three

(The observatory and the stairs leading up to it. Immediately following. CELESTE climbs the stairs, enters the observatory. A window is open; the curtains billow into the room. She closes the window. LE GENTIL steps out of the shadows.)

LE GENTIL: I thought you'd never come. Don't be afraid, it's only me.

CELESTE: Le Gentil?

LE GENTIL: Le Gentil, yes, in the flesh.

(He moves to the desk, lights a candle.)

CELESTE: How long have you been here?

LE GENTIL: I don't know. Hours.

CELESTE: Hours! But we've—

LE GENTIL: Come here by the light. I want to look at you.

CELESTE: We've been waiting for you!

LE GENTIL: Like vultures, I know. *(Lifts the candle.)* Come to the light, Celeste. You're not afraid, are you?

CELESTE: Of course not.

LE GENTIL: In that case, you won't mind if I look at you.

(She steps into the light. He studies her, lets out a breath.)

My God! My worst fear, come to pass.

CELESTE: What do you mean? What do you mean by that? And why do you call us vultures?

(LE GENTIL turns away, sets down the candle, begins to move restlessly around the room.)

LE GENTIL: This room! It's like a dream to me. And everything that happened here, a dream. We said goodbye here, didn't we? I seem to remember.

CELESTE: You *seem* to remember?

LE GENTIL: No, no, I remember. There was moonlight, wasn't there? It washed the room. You came to me half-dressed, and half asleep. You begged me to seduce you.

CELESTE: I wouldn't put it that way.

LE GENTIL: Oh yes, you came right out with it. I liked that. Damn near did it, too. You look confused. How could you forget these things? It's not so long ago.

CELESTE: Isn't it?

LE GENTIL: Well, is it?

CELESTE: Only six years!

LE GENTIL: Seems like yesterday to me. How is my mother?

CELESTE: Your mother?

LE GENTIL: My mother, yes.

CELESTE: She's waiting for you—

LE GENTIL: With all her faculties?

(CELESTE hesitates.)

No. I'm not surprised. Her letters have given her away. They used to be precise; they've grown quite winsome. Prepare me, Celeste. I want to know before I see her.

CELESTE: Some days her mind is very clear—

LE GENTIL: And some days foggy. *(Turns away.)* Like the sea.

CELESTE: You ought to see her. You ought to let her know you're here.

LE GENTIL: *(On the move.)* In time.

CELESTE: She's waited patiently for hours. We expected you at four, you see.

LE GENTIL: I know.

CELESTE: We had everything planned.

LE GENTIL: I'm sure you did, right down to the last painful detail. I'm sorry; couldn't face it. There's an odour of expectation in this place— not just in it, all around it, everywhere. I got wind of it as far away as Paris. Did you always stand like that?

CELESTE: Like what?

LE GENTIL: Never mind. Tell me about Demarais.

CELESTE: Demarais?

LE GENTIL: I want to know how he is.

CELESTE: He's—improving, I would say.

LE GENTIL: Thank God for that. Poor Demarais. I've never seen a man that sick, who lived. We damn near had to bury him at sea. There's nothing you could name he would have hated more. You're sure that he's improved?

CELESTE: Yes.

LE GENTIL: Good. Good for now, at least. He'll likely have a relapse, maybe several; that's the pattern. Your hair is different, isn't it? Darker. Or have you changed the style?

CELESTE: It's—

LE GENTIL: Darker, I would say. *(Turns away.)* Sit down.

CELESTE: I beg your pardon?

LE GENTIL: I said sit down.

(He begins to remove his jacket.)

CELESTE: I don't want to sit down.

LE GENTIL: Do it anyway.

CELESTE: Why should I?

LE GENTIL: Because I want you to. There's something about your attitude, the way you stand, the way you hold your arms. I don't care for it.

CELESTE: You don't—?

LE GENTIL: Care for it.

(He tosses his jacket across a chair.)

CELESTE: I don't give a damn if you care for it or not!

(He turns back to her.)

I don't know who you think you are, I don't know what you think you're doing. But if you expect me to stand here and put up with this—

LE GENTIL: Not at all. I expect you to sit here and put up with it.

(She turns to leave.)

Celeste! I'm teasing you. Surely you know that I'm teasing. *(Moves so that he can see her face.)* I had to do something, you looked so serious, as though the end of the world were at hand. It's not the end of the world for you, is it—my coming home?

CELESTE: Of course not.

LE GENTIL: Then why do you look as though it is?

CELESTE: It's because of the way you behave.

LE GENTIL: And how do I behave?

CELESTE: Oh! You're not going to pretend that you don't know.

LE GENTIL: But I don't.

CELESTE: You're constantly interrupting me. I've hardly been able to finish a single sentence! You leap from one subject to another— *(Breaks off.)* What are you grinning about?

LE GENTIL: Nothing.

CELESTE: I don't find any of this amusing.

LE GENTIL: I know. Go on, Celeste. I'm listening.

CELESTE: I think—from the time I walked in here, I think you've been quite rude.

LE GENTIL: Rude? *(Moves away.)* Nonsense. You're being much too critical.

CELESTE: *(Barely in control.)* I can't remember a time in this house when we've been able to have a conversation that didn't eventually, no matter what it was, come back to you. I can't remember an hour when your name wasn't mentioned. In six solid years, not one of us has gone to sleep at night without praying for your safety. And you come home, come sneaking home like a thief in the night, and call us vultures?

LE GENTIL: That was unfair.

CELESTE: It was more than unfair; it was cruel. We don't deserve that, any of us. And we don't deserve to have our plans thrown in our faces. Imagine hiding up here, all this time. Hours, you say! While we've—

LE GENTIL: It wasn't hours. I don't know how long it's been; not hours. I wanted to see you alone, Celeste. Is that so hard to understand? My God, I've dreamt this night with you a thousand times. Why would I want to share it?

CELESTE: *(Hesitates.)* That still doesn't explain why you'd call us vultures.

LE GENTIL: You mustn't take offence at that. It has nothing to do with you, it comes of feeling suddenly—caged. You have to try to think of what I'm used to, what I've had the blessed fortune to grow used to.

CELESTE: And what's that?

LE GENTIL: Infinity! Infinity, Celeste. No end to anything, in any direction—east, south, north, west, up, down, anywhere! Can you imagine it? Can you imagine what it does to a man's soul? I find … I find the land has a way of closing in on me, that's all. You can understand that, can't you? Well? Can you or not?

CELESTE: I think so.

LE GENTIL: Good. I was hoping that you could. Come here. *(Waits.)* Come here, Celeste. *(Laughs.)* You're not going to do it, are you?

CELESTE: No.

LE GENTIL: You won't sit down when you're told to, you won't come to me when you're called. What am I to understand from this?

CELESTE: I'm not a little girl anymore.

LE GENTIL: I can see that.

CELESTE: I won't be led around by the nose.

LE GENTIL: Is that how you remember it?

CELESTE: Precisely.

LE GENTIL: And I remember it the other way around. I remember being led by the nose. What do you make of that? One of us has to be wrong. *(Moves to her, takes her hand.)* Have a little pity on me, Celeste. No matter how we began, it wouldn't be as you'd imagined it. I was bound to disappoint you. Wasn't I?

CELESTE: Not necessarily.

LE GENTIL: Yes, I was, and I'll tell you why. You've forgotten me, Celeste—

CELESTE: No.

LE GENTIL: You have, you've forgotten the kind of man I am. You were expecting someone else, I think.

CELESTE: I was expecting—

LE GENTIL: Someone pale and sappy and sentimental. Why deny it? It's what comes of reading all those novels.

CELESTE: I don't read novels!

LE GENTIL: No? What do you read then, astronomy? Don't look for a story-book suitor, Celeste. You won't find him in me.

(They stare at one another. Several beats.)

CELESTE: The last thing on this earth I want—believe me!—is a story-book suitor.

LE GENTIL: Good; I'm glad to hear it. *(Lifts her hand, studies it.)* What do you want?

CELESTE: *(Fervently.)* A real one.

LE GENTIL: In that case, you must expect some imperfections. Am I right?

CELESTE: Of course.

LE GENTIL: Well then, that's understood. Your hair *is* darker, I'm convinced of it. It looks as rich as sable. *(Touches her hair.)* What are you thinking? Tell me.

CELESTE: You don't look at all like I remember.

LE GENTIL: No? How do I look?

CELESTE: I think you look—*(Breaks off.)*

LE GENTIL: Go on, say it.

CELESTE: You look quite foreign.

LE GENTIL: *(Laughs.)* Do I? Good.

CELESTE: No, I mean quite—wild.

LE GENTIL: *(Touches her face.)* Are you afraid of me?

CELESTE: A little.

LE GENTIL: I'm glad.

CELESTE: Why?

LE GENTIL: Because I find that I am terrified of you. *(To lighten the moment.)* It's the dress, I think.

CELESTE: The dress?

LE GENTIL: *(Steps back.)* The dress, yes, definitely. It's quite elaborate, isn't it? Almost like a wedding gown.

CELESTE: *(Tight.)* It's not at all like a wedding gown.

LE GENTIL: No? Well, what would I know? Where I've been, women don't bother much with clothes. Some of them don't bother with clothes at all. *(Watches her; laughs; moves away.)* I'm glad to see you still know how to blush, Celeste.

CELESTE: *(Under her breath.)* I wish I didn't.

LE GENTIL: *(Turns back.)* What did you say?

CELESTE: I said I wish I didn't, and I hope that soon I won't!

LE GENTIL: *(Smiles.)* I'd forgotten how candid you were about these things. I like that, Celeste.

CELESTE: Do you? I'm glad. I'm glad there's something about me that you like.

LE GENTIL: Something—? Oh, I see. *(Beat; turns away.)* If you really want to know what I think of you, I'll tell you. You put me in mind of a ship.

CELESTE: A ship?

LE GENTIL: A ship, a particular ship. I'll tell you about her, if you're interested. Maybe you're not.

CELESTE: I am.

LE GENTIL: She was called *La Marielle.* You can tell by her name what kind of ship she was. *La Marielle!* So many days at sea, so many ships; she stands out like a beacon. *(Begins to move.)* We were somewhere east of the Seychelles. You won't know where that is, it's—

CELESTE: Just north of Ile de France.

LE GENTIL: *(Turns to her.)* You did read my letters. I'm glad to hear it. I suppose you memorized them, too.

CELESTE: Of course not.

LE GENTIL: We were becalmed—had been for days; an eternity, it seemed. *(On the move.)* One morning I heard the captain say to the mate, "Look out for a squall today." I thought he must be joking. The sea was like a duckpond, not a cloud in the sky, not enough wind to blow a fly off the sails. At about mid-day a breeze sprang up; the sea began to swell and roll. The captain came running. He ordered all hands on deck, to make fast for a flying squall. They went up like a swarm of monkeys, but before they could finish the job, it was on us—a mountain of storm. It hit us with such force, it knocked *La Marielle* clean on her side. I thought we were lost. I did, by God, I thought for certain we were lost.

CELESTE: *(Beat.)* You didn't tell me this.

LE GENTIL: What? Oh no, I wouldn't have told you this. *(Begins to move closer.)* Well, she recovered herself. It took her a second or two but she did it, though she trembled from stem to stern. Her masts shook like young saplings. She weathered that squall, came through it as though she were charmed. What a beauty she was—sleek and lithe and limber. There weren't a handful of ships on the sea that could leave her astern. But for all her grace and speed and splendour, she had the heart of a man o' war. She haunts me, *La Marielle*. Are you jealous?

CELESTE: Of a ship?

LE GENTIL: It's no joke, Celeste. I'm in love with her.

CELESTE: When you left, you were in love with the sky.

LE GENTIL: I'm still in love with the sky. The sky, the sea, the tropics. I fall in love quite readily, it seems, but only with the truly splendid. Are you splendid, Celeste?

CELESTE: I'm afraid not.

LE GENTIL: You look splendid.

CELESTE: Do I?

LE GENTIL: Oh yes, you look like *La Marielle*. But are you like her? If you were knocked flat on your side by a flying squall, would you recover?

CELESTE: But I'm not likely to be, am I.

(He stares at her.)

I don't understand what you're trying to tell me. If you're saying that you don't want to marry me—

LE GENTIL: Of course I want to marry you. My God, haven't I come halfway round the world to do it?

CELESTE: Then—

LE GENTIL: I don't know how to explain it. Something happens, when you get out there, time ... dissolves. Weeks, months, days—these things don't exist. Only the moment exists, and the will to live it fully. You feel a little drunk, sometimes—you actually feel quite giddy—on the power of the moment. You feel as though your life is an odyssey, and that to live it less fully than you can would be a travesty. *(Beat; turns away.)* Listen to me. How can I expect you to understand? How can anyone understand odysseys when all they've known is needle-work?

(He moves to the window and stares out. CELESTE manages, with an effort, to control herself.)

CELESTE: This may come as a surprise to you, but I don't know the first thing about needlework.

LE GENTIL: No?

CELESTE: No. I don't do it, you see. I don't do any of it. I don't baste, I don't sew, I don't knit, I don't mend, I don't darn, I don't tat, I don't embroider and I do not—do—petitpoint!

(He turns to face her.)

I do, however, read. I can read, and because I can read I can learn. Oh, I can't actually travel—you have the advantage of me there—but I can read about travel, I can dream about it, I can imagine what it's like. I've been everywhere with you. You don't know it, but I have. I know every inch of sea you've sailed, every island you've set foot on. I know how the rains come sweeping across the mountains of Ile de France, and how the island itself lies curled in the sea like an oyster. I know about doldrums and trade winds and tides. Tides! Tides are so mysterious. We've known about them since the days of Alexander, yet there's so much we don't know. Why, for instance, there are two high and two low tides every day in some places, and only one in others. Why the tides of Saint-Malo rise almost ten metres and only a fraction of that on the islands you visited. They do; did you know that?

LE GENTIL: No.

CELESTE: I want to know why. I want to know everything there is to know, before I die. This was your gift to me, you see? You pointed me at the sky and said, look! And when I looked, what did I see? Mirrors! Mirrors reflecting mirrors reflecting mirrors, on and on into infinity. So much to know, so much to learn, so much to wonder about. Once you begin to wonder, it's impossible, isn't it?—inconceivable!—to abandon that sense of wonder for anything as straightforward and mundane as a needle and a piece of thread.

(Silence. CELESTE is almost as surprised as he is.)

LE GENTIL: My God, Celeste. I had no idea.

(Several beats. Suddenly he laughs.)

But this is wonderful. *(Moves to her.)* This is wonderful, Celeste! To think that you would do this! *(Laughs again.)* I can't tell you how delighted I am, I can't begin to tell you.

CELESTE: I was hoping you'd be pleased.

LE GENTIL: Pleased! There's nothing you could have done that would have pleased me more. This is wonderful, Celeste. This makes everything possible! Because once you know what it is to wonder, to have that *hunger—(Breaks off; takes her hands.)* I've travelled half the world, seen such beauty it would stun the mind. But I haven't seen anything, anywhere, which pleases me as much as you. Will you marry me, Celeste? Immediately? Without reservation?

CELESTE: Yes.

LE GENTIL: Yes! Good. Wonderful. Now. I want to know where you'd like me to take you. We're going away together, just the two of us. Where shall it be, Lyon? Provence? I want you all to myself from the day I marry you until the day I have to leave. We'll start a family. You wanted to do that before I went away the last time, remember? Well, this time we're going to do it. We'll start a family, and then when I come back—

CELESTE: Leave. You're going to leave? Of course you are, how stupid of me. This is what you've been saying all along, isn't it?

(She backs away, then turns and runs toward the exit.)

LE GENTIL: Celeste!

(He runs after her, steps in front, takes hold of her. She struggles to get free.)

Stop it. Stop it, Celeste. *(With authority.)* Stop it immediately!

(She obeys.)

Now sit down. *(Very shaken.)* Sit down, and we'll talk this through. Please, Celeste.

(She lets him lead her to a chair, and sinks into it. He pours a drink from a carafe and hands it to her.)

Take it. Take it, Celeste.

(She takes it.)

   Drink it.

(She does. He sits next to her.)

I've been doing some calculations. It occurred to me there had to be better places in the tropics for charting the transit than the one favoured by the Academy—better places than Pondichéry. I started doing some calculations, and I discovered I was right. In particular, there's a place called Manila. Unfortunately, it isn't ours; it's Spain's. Arrangements would have to be made with the Spanish Court—

CELESTE: *(Very flat.)* What does it matter. The transit is over. What does it matter now where the best place was?

LE GENTIL: I'm not talking about the last transit, I'm talking about the next one. The Academy wants someone in Pondichéry, since by the grace of God it happens to be French again, but—

CELESTE: *(Turns away.)* My God.

LE GENTIL: I'm making a bid for Manila. From Manila, a man could sail on to Mexico, down the coast of South America, around Cape Horn and home across the Atlantic. A complete circumnavigation of the globe!

CELESTE: *(Beat.)* You're going away again. You've just barely walked through the door, and you're going away.

LE GENTIL: Not immediately. Not for months.

CELESTE: How many months?

LE GENTIL: Eight, possibly ten. I intend to spend them all with you.

CELESTE: *(Beat.)* How long this time?

LE GENTIL: How long will I be gone? Three years.

> *(CELESTE laughs.)*

I swear to you, Celeste, on everything that's holy: three years, no more.

CELESTE: What if you miss it?

LE GENTIL: The transit? I won't.

CELESTE: You missed the last one.

LE GENTIL: That was because of the war. There's no war now, thank God.

CELESTE: What if it's cloudy?

LE GENTIL: That's unlikely, in Manila; that's the point.

CELESTE: What if it is? You'll be going back to chart the next one.

LE GENTIL: Definitely not.

CELESTE: You say that now.

LE GENTIL: There won't be another transit of Venus for more than a hundred years.

CELESTE: And you'd let that stop you?!

LE GENTIL: *(Beat.)* Try to understand, Celeste—

CELESTE: This will be the end of me.

LE GENTIL: Don't say that.

CELESTE: It will.

LE GENTIL: You'll ride right through it. You'll ride right through it and come out stronger, and more splendid, on the other side.

CELESTE: Oh! I see.

LE GENTIL: I know you have it in you. I'm counting on that.

CELESTE: I'm not a ship.

LE GENTIL: You know what I mean.

CELESTE: I'm not a bloody ship!

(She stands and moves away.)

LE GENTIL: Please, try to understand. I have to finish the work I started. I made a promise—

CELESTE: To me!

LE GENTIL: To my father, many years ago. For the love of astronomy, I broke that promise. What a terrible breach of trust! But if I can do something significant for the world, it will cancel out that broken promise. All I want—all I want, Celeste—is the chance to pull a single slender thread from the veil of ignorance we wear, that clouds our understanding of the universe, and of God. If God intended to deny me this work, why would He take me all that way, only to strand me on a ship at sea where I could watch the transit but not measure it? There had to be a reason, Celeste, and this is what it was: to ensure that I'd go back to chart the next one.

CELESTE: You can't be certain of that.

LE GENTIL: I am. I am certain. It was a sign. I wrestled with it for a long, long time, and finally I understood.

CELESTE: And what about your promise to me? Does that count for nothing?

LE GENTIL: But I've come back, Celeste. I'm going to marry you. And then, for a little while, I have to go away.

CELESTE: *(Several beats.)* Does Demarais know about this?

LE GENTIL: He knew I was considering it.

CELESTE: Of course! He's not going with you, though.

LE GENTIL: He shouldn't have come with me the first time.

CELESTE: Then take me. *(Faces him.)* Le Gentil? Take me with you when you go.

LE GENTIL: Come, Celeste—

CELESTE: I won't be any trouble. I've studied all of it. I know about the seas, and sailing. I know about the stars. You can teach me to assist you. I can help.

LE GENTIL: *(Stands.)* Absolutely not. It's dangerous, it's unhealthy. Look at Demarais.

CELESTE: Look at you.

LE GENTIL: No. *(Moves away.)* Definitely not. I'd never risk it.

CELESTE: Don't leave me. Don't go off and leave me again. Le Gentil—

LE GENTIL: For the love of Christ, stop calling me Le Gentil! My God, if you're going to marry me, don't you think it's time you moved up to something a little less impersonal?

(He moves to the windows. Several beats.)

CELESTE: There'll be no marriage.

LE GENTIL: Come, Celeste, you don't mean that.

CELESTE: I do.

LE GENTIL: You're only saying it because you're upset.

CELESTE: I need you, Guillaume. I don't know if you understand what that means, but I need you. *(Gradually losing control.)* Sometimes I can't sleep at night, for needing you. I'm sick to death of making do with dreams, and letters—and a phantom lover. I want a real lover! I want a husband, I want a family, I want a future. I don't want to be stuck on a shelf, like a book nobody bothers to read. I want to get started ... with my life!

LE GENTIL: *(Moves to her.)* And that's exactly what we're going to do; we're going to start your life. The only difference is that by next spring—

CELESTE: No, you don't understand. I need you here, Guillaume. Beside me. To help me be what I want to be.

LE GENTIL: And what's that?

CELESTE: What you are! I want to be—what you are. My life is an odyssey, too. Why must it be played out on such a tiny map?

(She is very upset. He moves closer.)

LE GENTIL: What would you have me do, stay home and grow miserable? Difficult to live with, impossible to please? Useless and idle?

CELESTE: You wouldn't have to be idle. You could find something to do.

LE GENTIL: Such as?

CELESTE: You could write your memoirs.

LE GENTIL: That's for old men.

CELESTE: You could—

LE GENTIL: I'm forty-one, Celeste. I'm strong and healthy. I still need what's difficult, to try my hand at, not what's easy. I need an idea in my mind large enough to scare the hell out of me. That's the only way I can function.

CELESTE: Don't leave me. I'm begging you—

LE GENTIL: Don't beg. Don't ever beg. I won't compromise, Celeste, I'm warning you

CELESTE: Neither will I.

LE GENTIL: If you persist in this foolishness, I won't linger here, trying to change your mind. I'll leave immediately.

CELESTE: Perhaps you should.

LE GENTIL: I can, quite easily. I can get a ship within a fortnight. I can be back in the tropics by Christmas.

CELESTE: That should make you very happy.

LE GENTIL: It will, believe me!

CELESTE: Then what are you waiting for? Do it! Do it, Guillaume. It will be easier for everyone.

(CELESTE turns abruptly and moves toward the exit. He stops her with a voice like thunder.)

LE GENTIL: Don't you dare walk out of here like this!

(She stops moving but doesn't turn.)

Don't you dare do this!

(Several beats; he struggles with himself.)

Don't—ask me—to choose! I can't choose. If I lose you, I lose my soul. If I don't go back, I won't know who I am. Celeste?

CELESTE: *(After a moment.)* How did this happen? I don't understand! Of the dream that was my life, this is the nightmare.

LE GENTIL: *(Moves to her.)* The transit takes place on the fourth of June. On the fifth, I'll start for home. That's a promise, Celeste. *(Beat.)* Will you wait for me? You must wait for me. Please. Give me something to dream about while I'm gone.

CELESTE: *(Beat.)* How do I know you'll ever want to stay? How do I even know you'll come back?

LE GENTIL: I'll come back. I will, Celeste. Because you and I—you and I are fixed by God in a kind of orbit. I circle round you like a planet round the sun. No matter how far I wander, you always draw me back. You always do, Celeste. You always do.

CELESTE: *(Several beats.)* There'll be no excuses this time. No delays. Once the transit is over, you must come straight home. I'll wait for you, but only on that condition. I won't go on forever, competing with the universe. I won't do it, Guillaume.

(He touches her face. She exits. Blackout. End of Act Two.)

Act Three: November 1771

(The sitting room. Afternoon. A pale wintry day. Everything is covered in sheets. LE GENTIL, wearing an overcoat, stands at a window. To the extent possible, he should appear much older than in Act Two. His face is grim, his manner abrupt. He seems to have lost much of the effervescence that once characterized his actions and attitudes. Although he forces his body to perform as it always has, those who know him well or watch him closely will detect the strain. Suddenly, MARGOT runs on, in a coat and hat.)

MARGOT: Le Gentil? Is it really you? What a shock you've given us! I thought my heart would stop. I didn't know whether to laugh or cry, when I got your note. I hardly dared believe it. Guillaume?

LE GENTIL: Where is she?

MARGOT: I beg your pardon?

LE GENTIL: Celeste, where is she?

MARGOT: I couldn't simply leave a message; you have to understand. I felt I had to speak to her in person. That's why I'm a little late, I—

LE GENTIL: She's coming, then.

MARGOT: I was interrupted again and again as I came through. You can't imagine the sensation you've caused. People kept running to their windows, crying, "Is it true, is it really true?" They're saying you've been raised from the dead. Like Lazarus!

LE GENTIL: But is she coming, Margot.

MARGOT: *(Hesitates.)* I'm not sure.

LE GENTIL: What does that mean?

MARGOT: Please. Try to understand the position you've put her in. It's not an easy thing, to face the dead. I'm sure—

(Seeing his face at close range startles her.)

I'm sure she'll find the strength to do what's right. You mustn't be impatient. The news is still so fresh.

LE GENTIL: Listen, Margot, there's something I have to know—now, this minute: is she married? Is she married, yes or no?

MARGOT: No.

LE GENTIL: No! God be thanked. She's not ill?

MARGOT: No.

LE GENTIL: Not married, and not ill. That's it, then; that's all I ask.

(He turns back to the window.)

MARGOT: *(Shudders.)* My goodness, the house is cold. It feels as though it's been closed up forever. *(Hesitates.)* Oh, Guillaume. Just look at you! You look as though you truly have been raised from the dead.

LE GENTIL: Nonsense. *(Moves away from the window.)* I'm a little tired from travel, nothing more. I had to come across the Pyrenees by goat-cart, if you can picture it.

MARGOT: Goat-cart?

LE GENTIL: Anything was preferable to the sea. Come and sit down, Margot, please. I want to talk to you.

(MARGOT obeys. He sits across from her.)

I've just come from my solicitor. My former solicitor, I should say; naturally, I dismissed him. He tells me that my mother has been sent away.

MARGOT: She's with her cousin in Lyon. We had no choice, you see. Once they decided that you must be dead—

LE GENTIL: I want you to go and bring her back.

MARGOT: When?

LE GENTIL: Immediately. Tomorrow.

MARGOT: Guillaume, I have another position now. I can't simply—

LE GENTIL: Give it up.

MARGOT: Give it up! Just like that?

LE GENTIL: Yes. You belong here, Margot. This is your home. If you like, I'll send a note to your employer. I'll tell him I've been raised from the dead; that ought to inspire him to oblige. What do you say to that?

MARGOT: I'm afraid it's not that simple.

LE GENTIL: *(An explosion.)* Margot, for the love of Christ, I am trying to put my life back together! Don't impede me!

MARGOT: *(Controls herself with an effort.)* Your life, Guillaume—your life is only one of several which have been quite drastically upset. You can't come walking in here after all this time and start demanding things. And expect us all to fall in line!

LE GENTIL: Margot, please try to understand. I've spent twenty-nine months trying to get home—twenty-nine months!—and everything has gone against me. Everything! And now—now, when I'm finally able to stand under my own roof—*(With a gesture that takes in the room.)*—look at it! Just look at it! In my worst nightmares, I never imagined I'd be coming back to this.

MARGOT: *(Beat; then quietly.)* How did it happen, Guillaume, that we didn't hear from you? The last letter Celeste has arrived a full two years ago.

LE GENTIL: *(Hesitates.)* For a time I couldn't write. I was ill.

MARGOT: Ill.

LE GENTIL: I was flat on my back for eight solid months. Couldn't find the strength to sit, let alone to write. Couldn't get out of India to save my soul! And when I did, when I finally got as far as Ile de France, it was only to fall ill again. Eventually, when I was well enough at last to go on, every ship I set foot on carried me into some fresh tragedy. One of them actually carried me into a hurricane. What an experience that was! I regard it as nothing short of a miracle that we were able to limp back to port, clutching our tattered sails and broken masts. *(Beat.)* I tried again and again to get away, set out in half a dozen ships; again and again I failed. It was a nightmare; it would not end. If anyone had told me a few years ago that the day would come when the sight of the sea would make me want to weep—*(Breaks off.)*

MARGOT: But why didn't you let her know, Guillaume? One letter! One letter, to say you were alive.

LE GENTIL: It's difficult to explain, I was—confused. I couldn't seem to find the will. And I kept thinking—well, perhaps tomorrow ...

MARGOT: You made a promise to Celeste. You broke that promise, and you didn't tell her why. You simply disappeared! It was as though the sea had opened up and swallowed you whole. And now you come along, at this late date, and you tell me that you couldn't seem to find the will!

LE GENTIL: *(Several beats.)* I was—ashamed. I used to know what I was meant to do. I was meant to unravel God's great mysteries! But I was wrong. *(Beat.)* Sometimes, Margot ... sometimes I still feel quite confused. I don't mean up here—*(Taps his forehead.)*—I mean in here. *(Taps his chest.)* I find myself, sometimes, staring at my hands ... *(With difficulty.)* I look back, and search my life, and it seems to me that in my confidence, in my supreme self-confidence, all I've brought to everyone I've loved, and been loved by, is pain. What a legacy! Clearly, I must set things right. But I don't—you see, this is the worst of it. I don't know if I'll ever be able to trust my judgement again.

MARGOT: *(Beat.)* Now listen to me, Guillaume. You've been very ill, you've had a long journey, you're exhausted. You must try not to dwell on these things. Once you've had a chance to recover your strength, you'll find your optimism will return as well.

LE GENTIL: You're very kind, Margot. Much kinder than I deserve. *(Without meeting her eyes.)* I'm afraid there was a time I may have caused you pain, as well.

MARGOT: If I denied that, I'd be denying that I ever cared for you. And that would be a lie. *(Choosing her words.)* I did care for you once, but I cared much more for Celeste.

(No response. He stares gloomily at his hands.)

LE GENTIL: I often thought of Demarais, while I was ill. I've been wanting to ask about him. I'm almost afraid to. Something tells me it hasn't gone well for him. You don't correct me.

MARGOT: No.

LE GENTIL: My God.

MARGOT: I'm afraid he—

LE GENTIL: No, don't tell me. There's only so much bad news a man can stomach in a day. *(He stands, moves away.)* You're right, you know. The house is cold. I've just begun to feel it.

MARGOT: Where will you stay tonight, Guillaume?

LE GENTIL: Here, of course.

MARGOT: You're staying in this empty house? No heat, no food—

LE GENTIL: I don't need either.

MARGOT: On the contrary, you need both, especially when you've been so ill. I think you should—

LE GENTIL: I'm staying here.

MARGOT: For heaven's sake!

LE GENTIL: I want my home restored to me. I want everything as it was, exactly. After what I've been through, I don't see how anyone can deny me that. *(Stands.)* You'll fetch my mother home tomorrow. If you need a letter, I will write one. In fact, I'll write it now.

(He moves to the desk, removes its cover, starts rummaging for writing materials.)

MARGOT: Guillaume. You've been gone a very long time. You can't simply reappear—suddenly, out of the blue—and expect everything to be the way it was.

LE GENTIL: Not immediately, perhaps, but I can make a start.

MARGOT: I'm afraid things may be a little more complicated than you realize.

LE GENTIL: Complicated! You sound like my solicitor. He's gone and sold off half the property—to pay my debts, he says. Debts! I've never been in debt in my life. People I haven't even heard of have laid claim to my estate. We're lucky to have furniture to sit on, and that's no exaggeration. And the worst of it, the cruelest blow of all, comes from the Academy. They've given away my seat, for God's sake. Imagine! After all the work I've done. This would never have happened if Delisle were alive. He would never—I'm quite certain ...

(He leans on the desk for support.)

MARGOT: *(Stands.)* What's the matter?

LE GENTIL: *(Waves her away.)* Nothing.

MARGOT: You don't look well at all.

LE GENTIL: I'm fine. Fine! *(Sinks into a chair.)* It's nothing. *(Meaning the letter.)* To whom do I address this?

MARGOT: There's no point in writing that now.

LE GENTIL: Why not?

MARGOT: I'll get it later, if I need it. If I decide to fetch your mother.

LE GENTIL: If you decide—?

MARGOT: I think you should prepare yourself, Guillaume. As many disappointments as you've had today, you should prepare yourself for more.

(CELESTE enters quietly, wearing a cloak or cape. At first, no one sees her. She stares at LE GENTIL; her face registers no expression at all.)

LE GENTIL: I know my mother's mind is gone. I know that. She needs attention night and day; that I know as well. I intend to see that she—

(LE GENTIL suddenly stands; he has seen CELESTE. He stares at her for some time. When he speaks again, his voice and manner are entirely changed.)

How do you do that? How do you manage to grow more and more beautiful while the rest of the world—grows grey?

(CELESTE holds his gaze but doesn't answer.)

Celeste?

(He moves towards CELESTE, but something in her attitude discourages him. He stops.)

I'm glad you've come. Your mother wasn't sure you'd do it. I knew you would, though I realize it's been a shock for you, to discover I'm alive. It's been a shock for me to discover I've been dead! Celeste?

MARGOT: Why don't you sit down, Celeste?

CELESTE: I dreamt this, all of it. I dreamt it over and over. Long after they said that you were dead, long after I'd forced myself to believe it, I dreamt you were alive, and had come back to me—just like this! And I stood here, staring at you. And I couldn't speak for pain.

MARGOT: *(Takes a step towards her.)* Celeste.

CELESTE: I couldn't understand it; it made no sense. Why not joy instead of pain? It was terrible; it always woke me up. And then I'd remember that you were dead, and none of it was true. It was an invention of the mind, echoing the agony of the heart. It was never meant to be true.

MARGOT: *(Moves to her.)* Come and sit down.

CELESTE: No. I can't stay.

MARGOT: I have to leave myself, quite soon. We'll walk back together.

(CELESTE allows MARGOT to lead her to a chair. She sits. MARGOT starts off.)

CELESTE: *(To MARGOT.)* Where are you going?

MARGOT: To lay out some blankets.

CELESTE: No, Mother—

MARGOT: He insists on staying here, and the house is very cold.

CELESTE: *(Quiet, emphatic.)* I need you here.

MARGOT: I know. I won't be long.

LE GENTIL: Is she all right?

MARGOT: She will be. Go gently with her, please.

> *(MARGOT exits. Beat.)*

LE GENTIL: My God, Celeste, I'm sorry. It didn't occur to me they'd take it into their heads to declare me dead. I hope you understand that. If I'd known they'd done that, I'd have ... I don't know what I would have done.

CELESTE: Well, it doesn't matter now.

LE GENTIL: You're sure?

CELESTE: I have what I want.

LE GENTIL: *(Unable to help himself.)* You look so beautiful! Just to look at you makes me feel thirty-five again.

> *(She turns away. He adopts a lighter tone.)*

What have you been doing, to become so beautiful?

CELESTE: *(Hesitates.)* What do you mean?

LE GENTIL: Nothing, I only meant—well, for instance, do you still like to read?

CELESTE: Not as much.

LE GENTIL: You're not still fascinated with the tides?

CELESTE: Not really.

LE GENTIL: What do you do then, with your time?

CELESTE: *(Smiles.)* Needlework.

LE GENTIL: *(Grins.)* Seriously, now.

CELESTE: *(Seriously.)* Needlework.

> *(He has no idea what to make of this. He takes a package from his pocket.)*

LE GENTIL: I have a gift for you, Celeste. I hope you'll accept it. *(Again, striving for lightness.)* If not, I'll have to find some other woman to give them to, and I don't know any who could wear them half as well as you.

(He offers her the package. She stares at it but doesn't take it.)

Combs, for your hair. Tortoise-shell. Very beautiful, I think. From the Celebes.

CELESTE: I'm sorry. *(Not unkindly.)* I don't wear combs.

LE GENTIL: I see. Well, I—have other gifts. In fact, I have a chest full but it hasn't yet arrived. I sent it on by ship from Cadiz. Silks and cottons; fine lace and spices. Fans, jewels, carvings. Celeste?

CELESTE: It's odd, isn't it, to be sitting here? I didn't expect to see this room again. Your mother would be so impressed!

LE GENTIL: With what?

CELESTE: With your escape. From the deep. We thought you'd drowned, you see.

LE GENTIL: I know.

CELESTE: We saw you lying at the bottom of the sea, your bones picked clean long since by little fish. We found it easier to think of you that way. We had a lot in common, your mother and I.

LE GENTIL: I'm going to bring her home, Celeste, as soon as possible. Look after her—

CELESTE: We grieved you together, the three of us. Your mother, my mother and I. Never was a man so well-wept!

(He sits next to her.)

LE GENTIL: I wanted to get home, Celeste. More than anything else, more than anything in the world, I wanted to get home to you. I'd have walked the oceans, if I could have.

CELESTE: No, don't say this. I don't want any explanations.

LE GENTIL: Celeste, you have to let me explain—

CELESTE: *(Very firm.)* No. I don't have to. And if you insist, I will leave immediately.

LE GENTIL: Celeste, for pity's sake—

CELESTE: *(To finish it.)* You got your measurements; what else matters?

LE GENTIL: I—

CELESTE: *(Quotes from memory.)* "The nights at Pondichéry are of the greatest beauty. You cannot imagine how stunning is the sky that falls around me on these perfect, scented nights." You remember that, I'm sure. *(Again, from memory.)* "Today the wind is from the southeast, a good omen. This wind is called the broom of the coast, and always brings serenity." That was early on the morning of the transit. So you got your measurements, all right, but you weren't ready to come home—*(Starts to lose control.)*—for whatever reason—

LE GENTIL: Celeste—

CELESTE: That's why the letters stopped. And if that's not true, then I don't want to know the truth. The truth is certain to be terrible.

LE GENTIL: In all these months, I have been engaged in a kind of struggle—with myself, and also, in a way, with God. I thought, you see—I always believed—that God had hidden His most precious secrets where they would be most difficult to find. I would look at the sky, or the sea—

CELESTE: I don't want to hear this.

LE GENTIL: Or the brooding hulk of a continent, and know that there the challenge lay. It didn't occur to me to look elsewhere—

CELESTE: I don't want to hear this!

LE GENTIL: *(Stands.)* It didn't occur to me that perhaps He had created all those things for another reason—

CELESTE: I don't want to know anything! I have it all constructed in my mind, and I won't allow you to get in there again and tear it down. I won't allow it!

LE GENTIL: *(Beat.)* I'm to be condemned without a trial, is that it? Even the worst of criminals—

    (MARGOT enters.)

MARGOT: There, that's done. Though I still think it would be wiser— *(Breaks off.)* Did I interrupt?

LE GENTIL: Yes!

CELESTE: No! *(To MARGOT.)* We have nothing to say that can't be said in front of you. Is that not so, Guillaume?

LE GENTIL: I don't wish to be rude, but—

CELESTE: *(To MARGOT.)* There, you see? He doesn't wish to be rude.

LE GENTIL: Celeste, we have so much to say to one another, so much to talk about. I want to get to know you again. I want to know everything about you. Whether you still dream of me. Do you, Celeste?

CELESTE: In a manner of speaking.

LE GENTIL: What does that mean?

CELESTE: *(Faces him.)* I see you at the bottom of the sea—a skull with gaping holes where the eyes once hung, a space inside the skull so vast and inhospitable no thought can linger there. No thought of any kind: of Venus, or of India; of the sky, or ships, or tides; and certainly no thought of me. I like that. I like to think of all that space within your skull and nothing flowing through it but the sea ... and now and then a fish.

    (Again, LE GENTIL is stunned into silence.)

MARGOT: Try to understand, Guillaume. She's been through so much.

LE GENTIL: *(To CELESTE.)* If you could only hear yourself! You talk as though you're sorry I'm alive.

CELESTE: Not for your sake; not at all. *(Strives for a light note.)* I feel a little sorry for the fish.

LE GENTIL: What kind of talk is this?! I have not come ten thousand leagues, with death clinging to my coat tails, to listen to talk like this!

MARGOT: Try to be patient, Guillaume.

LE GENTIL: *(To CELESTE.)* What do you expect me to do, for God's sake, apologize for staying alive?

MARGOT: Of course not.

LE GENTIL: Celeste?

CELESTE: *(Faces him.)* I don't know what your plans are, or your expectations—

LE GENTIL: The hell you don't.

CELESTE: The reason I've come here ... is to tell you that I'm going to have a child. I'm very happy about this, and I hope you'll do me the great courtesy of being happy for me.

    (Silence; it seems to go on forever.)

LE GENTIL: Whose child?

CELESTE: Pardon me?

LE GENTIL: Whose—child are you expecting?

CELESTE: Does it matter?

LE GENTIL: For the love of Christ!

CELESTE: I don't believe it matters.

LE GENTIL: You don't believe it matters! It looks to me as though it's the father who doesn't believe it matters.

CELESTE: Nothing could be farther from the truth.

LE GENTIL: Well, where is he, then? Doesn't he know where his duty lies? What kind of man is this?

CELESTE: *(Faces him.)* A gentle man.

LE GENTIL: A gentleman! He's no gentleman. If that was my child in your belly, if I was its father—

CELESTE: But it isn't. And you aren't.

> *(Stand-off. Several beats.)*

LE GENTIL: I want to meet the father.

CELESTE: You can't.

LE GENTIL: I insist on meeting him!

CELESTE: It's not possible.

LE GENTIL: Why not?

MARGOT: The father is dead. He intended to marry Celeste, but she delayed. And now he's dead.

LE GENTIL: That sounds like a story to me.

MARGOT: Guillaume—

LE GENTIL: It sounds like the sort of story people invent to protect the honour of a woman who has none.

CELESTE: *(Turns on him.)* That's right, I have no honour. Thank God for that. I never much liked it, anyway.

LE GENTIL: I know that well enough. You were always trying to give it away.

CELESTE: All I needed was a man who cared enough to take it!

MARGOT: Stop it, both of you! You're not going to tear each other into little pieces, not in my presence. I'm not going to let that happen, do you understand? Now. I want you to sit down, Celeste.

CELESTE: No.

MARGOT: You are going to sit down and you are going to do it now.

> *(CELESTE obeys. MARGOT turns to LE GENTIL.)*

I understand how difficult this is for you. But you must remember that in her condition—

LE GENTIL: I'm sorry.

MARGOT: Your very presence is a shock to her. I can't allow you to go on this way. If you persist, I'll take Celeste away from here immediately. Do you understand?

LE GENTIL: Of course.

>   *(Several beats. LE GENTIL turns to CELESTE.)*

Forgive me, Celeste. I had no right to say that.

CELESTE: *(Without looking at him.)* It's I who should apologize. I'm sure there was a better way to tell you, but for the life of me I couldn't think of it.

LE GENTIL: *(After a moment.)* When is the baby due, Celeste?

CELESTE: April.

LE GENTIL: And what are your plans?

CELESTE: I have a little money now, left me by the father—

LE GENTIL: A *little* money.

CELESTE: *(To finish it.)* Enough.

LE GENTIL: *(Takes a step towards her.)* Listen, Celeste—

CELESTE: I'm going to emigrate. To New France.

LE GENTIL: New France! You can't be serious.

CELESTE: I am. As soon as the child is old enough to travel.

LE GENTIL: Margot?

MARGOT: *(Moves in behind CELESTE.)* She's had this notion in her head the last few months. Nothing will dislodge it.

CELESTE: That's right.

MARGOT: *(To CELESTE.)* If you go, I intend to go with you.

>   *(Takes her hand.)*

LE GENTIL: And what exactly do you expect to do, in that wilderness?

CELESTE: Begin my life. It will be easy enough out there to pass myself off as a widow; no one will question it. I hope to get a position as a governess, perhaps even as a teacher. It's a rough place, but it has a future. And I want my child to have a future.

LE GENTIL: *(Moves next to her.)* Listen to me, Celeste. These plans of yours, they may have been necessary when you thought that I was dead. They're not necessary now.

CELESTE: They are.

LE GENTIL: No, they're not. I want to marry you, Celeste. I don't care who the father is, don't care if he's alive or dead; it's irrelevant to me.

I'm asking you, in all humility, to be my wife. After all this time—
eleven years, eight months and thirteen days—it still gives me more
pleasure to look at you than at anything else in the world.

CELESTE: *(Fighting back tears.)* Do you see, Mother? See how it is?
What are you going to do with a man like this? This man! This man
never learns when to come and when to go and when to simply—stay
away!

LE GENTIL: Tell me you'll marry me, Celeste.

CELESTE: It's too late, Guillaume.

LE GENTIL: No, I won't accept it. I won't allow you to do this. I will not
allow you to throw away your future, and mine as well, because of
one fateful indiscretion.

CELESTE: One—? No, you don't understand.

MARGOT: *(Quietly.)* Let it go, Celeste.

CELESTE: At first I went to him—simply to talk about you. He'd been
with you through so much, he knew you so well. It was almost as
though by touching him I could reach you. And I didn't just love him
a little bit; I loved him with everything I had. I loved him … the way
I'd wanted to love you. I had him for seven months. Seven months!
It seems to be my fate—to fall in love with men who go away.

(LE GENTIL sinks into a chair.)

MARGOT: *(To LE GENTIL.)* He caught pneumonia a few months ago.
He'd had so many relapses; each one left him weaker than the last. It
was inevitable. The physician said as much.

CELESTE: I grieved you, Guillaume. From the moment I understood
that you would break your promise, long—long!—before they said
that you were dead, I grieved you! And our lost love, and our lost
future. I wanted that future so badly! But finally I understood that I
would never have it. It wasn't meant to be. Once I understood that, I
was able to let you go. It wasn't easy, but I did it. And there's no going
back for me now, Guillaume. I can't go back. It's finished.

(CELESTE exits. Silence.)

LE GENTIL: I never believed I'd lose her. When I missed the first
transit, even after I missed the second she was always there. She
shone for me, in the distance, like the sun.

MARGOT: What are you saying, Guillaume? You missed the second
transit? But the conditions were ideal. According to your letter …

LE GENTIL: I heard the sand-bar moaning from the southeast, early on the morning of the transit. This made me think the wind was still from that direction. I was elated. This wind is called the broom of the gods, and it always—*(Breaks off.)* Did I say the gods? I meant the coast. It's called the broom of the coast, and it always brings serenity.

MARGOT: Yes?

LE GENTIL: I was mistaken. The wind had changed. The sky was covered everywhere in cloud. And in Manila, where I would have been if I'd had my way, the skies were perfectly clear.

(MARGOT doesn't know what to say. Finally, she moves to him.)

MARGOT: I have to go, Guillaume—to see that she gets safely home. There are beggars everywhere these days, and they seem to prey on women. Guillaume?

(No response. MARGOT hesitates, torn between staying and going. Finally, she exits. LE GENTIL sits motionless for a very long time. Blackout. The end.)

Non-fiction
Dramatic Body, The Jetsmark/Brask
Hot Ice: Shakespeare In Moscow, A Director's Diary Sprung/Much
Women on the Canadian Stage: The Legacy of Hrotsvit
Rita Much (Ed.)

Drama Anthologies
Airborne: Radio Plays by Women (The Morningside Dramas)
Ann Jansen (Ed.)
Dangerous Traditions: A Passe Muraille Anthology
Judith Rudakoff (Ed.)
Endangered Species Margaret Hollingsworth
On The MAP: Scenes from Manitoba Plays Rory Runnells (Ed.)
Take Five (The Morningside Dramas) Dave Carley (Ed.)

Drama
Amigo's Blue Guitar Joan MacLeod
Beautiful Lake Winnipeg Maureen Hunter
Bordertown Café Kelly Rebar
Chinese Man Said Goodbye, The Bruce McManus
Darling Family, The Linda Griffiths
Democracy John Murrell
Departures and Arrivals Carol Shields
Exile Archie Crail
Fire Paul Ledoux & David Young
Footprints on the Moon Maureen Hunter
Gravel Run Conni Massing
Invention of Poetry, The Paul Quarrington
Mail Order Bride, The Robert Clinton
Memories of You Wendy Lill
Midnight Madness Dave Carley
Mirror Game Dennis Foon
Oldest-Living, The Pat Smith
Particular Class of Women, A Janet Feindel
Prairie Report Frank Moher
refugees Harry Rintoul
Sky Connie Gault
Soft Eclipse, The Connie Gault
Steel Kiss Robin Fulford
Third Ascent, The Frank Moher
Transit of Venus Maureen Hunter
Unidentified Human Remains and the True Nature of Love Brad Fraser
Writing With Our Feet Dave Carley